Unlocked Keys for Godly Living

Unlocked Keys for Godly Living

Taya—
May God continue to enrich you
and use you mightily
Angela

Angela Thornton

© Copyright 2012 Angela Thornton

All rights reserved. This book is protected under the copyright laws of the United States of America. No portion of this book may be reproduced in any form, without the written permission of the publisher. Permission granted on request.

Unlock Publishing House
231 West Hampton Place
Capitol Heights, MD 20743
www.unlockpublishinghouse.com
1 (240) 619-3852

Edited by Ashley Brinkley

Cover design by Dwayne Moore (Beyond Human Media)

ISBN: 978-0-9855261-3-9

Scripture references are from the
New American Standard Bible (NASB) (1977)

Dedication

This book is dedicated to:

my beloved mother, Dotti Wynn, and
my dad, the late Rev. Samuel Hunter,
without whom I would not be here.

Acknowledgments

To my dear friend Barbara Woods, all I can say is thank you. You were patient, kind and a living epistle before me. You lived the Bible you spoke of, and as a result, I accepted Christ as my Savior. And yes, it was you, lo those many nights who prayed for me and who taught me how to pray effectively. To Bishop Ronald Kimble, you will never know the impact you have had on my spiritual growth and maturity. It was at the Life Center where I received Christ and really heard the gospel preached in such a way that it was illuminated in my mind, revealed in my spirit and became so real to me that it became my life's mission to apply the Word to every area of my life.

To Elder Jackie Rice, you were the first person to say God can use you. I vividly remember our conversation while I was your student assistant and you spoke life to the gift of teaching in me. I appreciate you. To Pastor Tejado Hanchell, as the then Assistant Dean of Calvary Bible Institute, you gave me my first opportunity to teach. To all my students, thank you for believing in me, especially during my early days of teaching. Stephen Contee, you honored and blessed me more than you know with your quiet, but intense desire to learn more about God and the faith you had in my ability to impart the truth of God's Word. To my pastors Bishop Alfred and Co-Pastor Susie Owens, you have poured abundant blessings in my life through your preaching, teaching, praying and loving spirits. Through you, I know what an excellent spirit in ministry, marriage and life should be. Thank you for being transparent, real and above all, holy examples of godly leadership.

Ashley, the editor of all editors, you are a jewel. Thanks for putting up with the myriad edits and changes. Dawn, mere words are not enough. I cannot imagine ever going through this process with any publisher other than you! This is only the beginning of great things for Unlocked Publishing House. I am so excited to watch the world get to know the phenomenal woman of God and publisher you are. You are anointed and called to this work.

To Kemba and Rosetta ... I appreciate your many hours of praying for and with me and all the hours we sat around my table organizing and reorganizing the Wise Words. Your initial edits and input were invaluable, your friendship immeasurable and your support intangible. I could not have completed this without you.

To my mom: Dotti Wynn, where do I begin? You have been my inspiration and my motivation. I could not have had a more fierce advocate and protector than you. The life you provided for Andre' and me did not come without sacrifice on your part and I will always be grateful to you for the sacrifices you made. Prayer, hard work and preparation were your mainstay and it is how I have patterned my life. I love you.

To Daniel, my husband, lover, confidant and friend, words cannot begin to explain all that you mean to me. It was during your prayer for me that March evening in 2009 that I heard the words Wise Word Wednesday. By the time you had finished, the Lord had given me the entire narrative for Peace, the first "Wise Word." You have always been my #1 cheerleader, chief encourager, shoulder to cry on and sounding board. You tell me I can when I feel I can't. You see gifting in me that I would never have thought possible. In a word, you Daniel L. Thornton encapsulate and embody all that the term "husband" means, for you really are my priest, provider, protector and gift from God.

Foreword

Angela, I love how you start with affliction because so many of us face it every day but, as you pointed out, affliction can bring us closer to God. It usually does!! Sometimes it can take affliction for us to wake up and realize He is there! I also like how you write about blessing the Lord. So many seek blessing from Him yet we forget we should be blessing Him as well! The format you use and the addition of the Scriptures at the end "key" is excellent. It allows people to go and get into God's word and find understanding on the topics you are writing about without just telling them the Scripture! I love to read books, but I feel that those who just spell out Scripture constantly throughout the book take away from the intimacy a person can find by picking up the Bible, finding the Scripture, and reading it themselves. You have a great book here!

Jane Reed, Editor-in-Chief
Blessed Life Magazine

ꞵ | ꞵ

Finally, finally, finally it's here, a spiritual word guide that takes the words of God and brings them to life. *Unlocked Keys for Godly Living* helps us understand with simplicity key spiritual words, their relevance to our lives and how to effectively apply them as 21st century Christians.

Dr. M. Lisa Robinson

ꞵ | ꞵ

Unlocked is a timely piece of work desperately needed in the body of Christ. The beauty of this book is it equips you with the ONE word that you need at that right moment in your life that could change your atmosphere, and ultimately your life. It only takes ONE word to do this. This book allows you to become a scholar of the Word of God, one word at a time, in a way that the Word becomes a part of your everyday vernacular and begins to effect change in your lifestyle that then effects change in your surroundings.

Dr. Shimere A. Williams

ᴄ঩ | ঵ᴐ

My experience with Angela's Wise Word is similar to my experience with southern cooked grits. You can enjoy it at any time and it goes with everything! I listen to the Wise Word Wednesday Live sessions and check out her blog to catch up on anything I've missed. Angela has a gift for taking heavy topics, breaking them down, and making it easy to understand and apply. I can't wait to read her new book! I know it will truly bless God's Kingdom.

Natasha Beene

ᴄ঩ | ঵ᴐ

I remember reading my first Wise-Word Wednesday and thought I think she's on to something. Today, I believe my thought is a reality. The reading of these Wise Words gave me hope on many days. It uplifted my spirit and made my heart sing. It made me see God in a totally different light. I would recommend the reading of this book to anyone who needs a life change. It literally changed my life. It changed me. Thanks Angela!

Blessings and Peace

Ellie Holliday

ଔ | ଓ

 To unlock a thing is to gain unfettered access to what lies behind the door. In *Unlocked Keys for Godly Living*, Angela Thornton gives the reader insight and revelation on how to successfully navigate the road to living a godly life. She clearly and simply dissects "keys" found throughout the Bible in short and powerful devotionals that encourage and empower you to seek God's will and His way. I am proud to recommend this book, written by my spiritual daughter of almost 20 years.

Archbishop Alfred A. Owens, Jr,
Presiding Prelate
Mt. Calvary Holy Churches of America
Washington, DC

Table Of Contents

Affliction... 17
Believe 21
Bible 25
Blessing 29
The Blood 35
Faith 39
Fasting.. 43
Favor.. 47
Fire 51
Friend 55
Gift... 61
God 65
Heart... 69
Heaven 73
Holiness 77
Holy Spirit.. 81
Honor.. 85
Jesus 89
Joy.. 93
Justification 97
Keep.. 101
Life.. 105
Love 109
Mercy 113
Name 117
Peace.. 121
Power and Authority... 125
Praise 129
Prayer 133
Promise 139
Purpose 143
Satan 147
Sin 151

Temptation 155
Think 159
Tongue 163
Tribulation 167
Trust 171
Wait 175
Wisdom 181
Worship 185
Worry 189

Affliction

Key Scripture: This is my comfort in my affliction, that Your Word has revived me. ~Psalm 119:50

Affliction is not generally the topic of dinner conversation. No one willingly wakes up and says, I think today, I'd like some affliction in my life. Yet, it is something that cannot be avoided, no matter how hard we try. Your salvation, great anointing or spectacular gifts cannot exempt you from affliction. You may operate in the entire five-fold ministry, but be assured trouble, trials, tribulation and suffering are coming your way. However, you can take comfort that the God of all flesh promises to deliver you from them all.

Sometimes affliction is simply the common lot of man. Sometimes it is constructive. Though we may not like it, affliction can also be corrective. Paul states suffering produces perseverance; perseverance, character; and character, hope. Some affliction is given only to glorify God in it and by it. The afflictions of the man born blind were of this nature. Jesus explained that he had been suffering neither for his own sin nor that of his parents, but only "that the work of God might be displayed in his life." Some afflictions are cosmic. Job was afflicted that Satan and the angels would know man can love and trust God for who He is and not merely for what He offers.

Affliction can and often does bring us closer to God. Without question, our prayer life increases. We learn to praise the Lord, even in the midst of the trial. Our worship becomes more intense as we seek the only wise God who is able to save and deliver us from destruction. We must remember our response to the

18

affliction is often a more valuable lesson than the actual problem. If we learn to respond as Job did and trust God, even when we don't see, feel, or hear God, we can bear the burden with joy, knowing that He who created us is able to deliver us.

For Christians, there is always hope and joy beyond the suffering. We must believe that God does not expect us to enjoy suffering. This is evidenced by the fact that our afflictions are always tempered by God's mercy. Even Jesus asked if the cup could be passed from Him. However, if we are not rooted and grounded in the Word, when tribulation and affliction arise, we will wither away.

Like the Savior, we must always say nevertheless, not my will but Your will be done. For the Psalmist tells us that many are the afflictions of the righteous, but the Lord will deliver him out of them all.

Please understand, Satan cannot afflict you without the Sovereign One's permission. God is always in control of your situation, just as He was in control of Job's and the circumstances surrounding his troubles. He is the same God today as He was then. More important, He is no respecter of persons.

What He did for Job and the children of Israel, the Lord can and will do for you. Take comfort, Jehovah Shammah is there, He is your refuge, your strength and your strong tower. Understand that your life is not a script to be passively followed. You must choose to obey, even when doing so will lead to affliction. Yet, you have a promise that the sufferings of this present age are not worthy to be compared to the glory which shall be revealed in us. Again, you are reminded that He, who has begun this good work in you, is well able to complete it until the day of Jesus Christ.

References: NASB; Boice Cmy; NASB Topics; Handbook of Bible Application

Scriptures: Ex 1:12; 3:17; Dt. 26:7; 1 Ki 8:35; Job1:6-2:7; 5:7; 13:15; 36:15; Psa 25:18; 34:19; 78:38-39; 119:22; 153; Prov 15:15; Eccl 6:2; Lam 1:3; Isa 53:4, 7; Amos 6:14; Nah 1:2; Matt 13:21; Lk 22:41-42; Jn 9:3; Rom 5:3-4; 8:18; 1 Cor 10:13; 2 Thess. 1:4; Jas 1:2-4; 1Pet 4:16, 19

Believe

Key Scripture: *Therefore I say to you, all things for which you pray and ask, believe that you have received them and they will be granted. ~Mark 11:24*

The Apostle's Creed is beautifully stenciled on wooden plaques in churches and printed in bulletins for recitation each Sunday. As eloquent as those words are, the question remains, do we really believe all that is written therein? Do we believe that God is the Father Almighty, maker of heaven and earth? Do you really know in whom you have belief?

Christ is talked about and often served, but is He really believed? Scripture admonishes us to believe in both the Father and the Son. God never called us to believe man. He commanded that we believe in Him through His Son. Jesus says, "He who believes in Me, does not believe in Me but in Him who sent Me." Belief in God requires us to believe that He is and that He rewards those who diligently seek Him.

By choosing to believe in Jesus, we can affect the destiny of our entire family. If we are to believe in God, we must also believe Him to be of infinite wisdom, sovereignty and power. In fact, one of the first things you must believe about God is that you belong to Him. As such, you act accordingly, acknowledging that in Him you move, breathe and have your very being.

In The Christian's Secret of a Happy Life, Hannah Smith says if a man does not believe that the entire world is as God's family, where nothing happens by chance, but all is guided and directed by the care and providence of the Creator of the universe, then he cannot be said truly to believe in God. Real belief requires faith in more than what you see. Because he believed God, Abraham was willing to sacrifice his son even though there was no evidence that Jehovah would step in and save Isaac.

Throughout Scripture we find salvation is freely given. God's limitless love is declared; while, forgiveness and justification are proclaimed. Until we believe, neither salvation that is freely given, God's declared love or His proclaimed forgiveness will ever be ours. Too often, we languish in a state of hearing the Word, knowing the Word, and attempting to live our lives for Christ, yet not fully believing the Word. The result is unbelief that festers as a canker sore and causes you to live beneath your privilege in Christ.

Believe that your sins are forgiven now (not at some future time and place) so that you may have joy and rest in God's peace. Believe because He is willing and able to do exceeding abundantly above all you could ever ask or think. Believe because Christ died for your sins. Believe because He yet lives. Believe because you have an assurance that the risen Savior is coming back again.

Believe because Heaven is your eternal home.

We must believe to see the goodness of the Lord in the land of the living. Believe that what He shows, He gives; what He is, He imparts. In your weakest moment, hold on and believe in the divine grace, mercy, favor and strength of God. If you believe the truth, you shall be saved. If you believe the lie, you shall surely be lost. For what you believe will be the catalyst of your greatest deliverance or your most resounding defeat! Whose report will you believe?

References: NASB; A Serious Call to a Devout and Holy Life; The Christian's Secret of a Happy Life; Holiness

Scriptures: Gen 22:1-13; Isa 43:6; Jn 3:18; 12:44; 17:11-23; Acts 2:21; 16:31; Rom 4:3; 10:-9-10; Eph 1:13; Heb 11:6; 1 Jn 5:13

Bible

Key Scripture: *All Scripture is inspired by God and profitable for teaching, for reproof, for correction, for training in righteousness; so that the man of God may be adequate, equipped for every good work. ~2 Tim 3:16-17*

Every industry, group, organization and religion has its own version. It has no equal and it has withstood the test of time and history. It is God's perfect and everlasting manifesto. Without it man would be lost. It is God's cleansing agent and it was written at His command. It is called by many names: the Word, the Law, Sword, Holy Scriptures, the Book of Truth and simply The Bible. In short, the Bible is God's inerrant, incontestable and infallible Word that is able to save your soul.

God's Book has many purposes. It is the vehicle by which He speaks to man. Within its pages, we find guidance, instruction, rebuke, comfort, assurance, enlightenment, and salvation. Its words offer life, hope and inspiration. We are preserved through it and edified by it. God the Father is explained; Christ, the Savior is revealed and the Holy Spirit is promised.

We are admonished in Scripture to study to show ourselves approved. God knows the thoughts, plans and will for your life. He reveals those plans in the Bible. If you are to live in the fullness of all God has ordained for your life, you must fill your soul, feed your spirit and renew your mind with the Word of the Lord. Daily reading, meditating and study are required. Only then can you walk as you ought. Only then can you clearly see the way in which you should

go. Only then will you know the expecta
Father has of you. If read and studied, the
become as relevant to your life as breathing. It will
become the most important part of your spiritual
arsenal. It is the weapon you will use to confuse and
thwart the enemy's plans.

Confessing the words found within will give you
strength and power. Hiding its words in your heart
and allowing it to become a light to your feet and a
lamp unto your path will decrease your inclination to
sin. Believing its report will increase your faith and
trust in God. Obeying its laws, precepts and
commands will bring you in connection with God's
peace, prosperity, productivity (fruitfulness) and plan
(direction). To the obedient, God promises to bless
your going out and your coming in. He promises to
bless you in the city and in the field. You will be the
head and not the tail; above and not beneath.
Obedience to the commands of the Bible is better than
sacrifice. Conversely, ignoring and disobeying the
Word will cause the Father to chastise, rebuke, judge,
curse and unleash His wrath upon you.

The Bible can preserve you from ruin, empower
you to turn from sin and enable you to live holy. In his
description of the Bible, noted pastor and intercessor
Smith Wigglesworth calls the Bible supernatural in
origin, eternal in duration, inexpressible in valor,
infinite in scope, regenerative in power, infallible in
authority, universal in interest, personal in application
and inspired in totality.

The Bible: read it through, write it down, pray it
in, work it out, and pass it on.

27

References: NASB; NLT Verse finder;
Baker Topical Guide to the Bible

Scriptures: Ex 3:14; Dt 11:26-28; 28:1-
26; Ps 18:30; 119:4-6, 11; 89; 105; Isa
55:8; Jer 29:11; Matt 22:32; Jn 17:17;
Rom 1:2; 1Cor 2:12-16; Gal 3:10; Eph
6:17; 2Ti 2:15; 3:16

Blessing

Key Scripture: *All these blessings will come upon you and overtake you if you obey the Lord your God. ~Dt. 28:2*

We all desire the blessings of the Lord. We sing about them. Books are written about being blessed. We stand in prayer lines to have blessings bestowed upon us and too often we give in to the latest schemes, scams, and programs to garner God's blessings. Yet, we must understand that God's blessings are neither mysterious nor can they obtained by human machination. You cannot bribe, trick, bully or manipulate God into blessing you.

If God's blessing is what you desire, a holy and faithful lifestyle is the cost. As a side note, we must understand that breathing God's air every day is a blessing. However, there are some blessings that go far beyond the ordinary and continue on for generations. For example, through Abraham, all the nations of the earth are blessed because he obeyed the Father's voice. Hence as a joint heir with Christ, we are recipients of the blessings of Abraham.

As redeemed believers, we have a right to expect our Master's blessings. Throughout Scripture, God promises to bless us. He promises to bless those who bless us. His word says we are blessed above all people. The Almighty's eternal covenant assures us that He is not a man that He should lie, neither is He the son of man that He should repent; for if He spoke it, He shall perform it. We can therefore boldly stand firm on His Word and proclaim that:

1.   We are blessed in the city and blessed in the field

2.   The blessings of the Lord make us rich and add no sorrow to us;

3.   The Lord has commanded His blessings on our storehouses; and

4.   All that we set our hands to is blessed

We must also understand that God's blessings are reserved for those He is in covenant relationship with. In the O.T., God's pronouncements of blessing were not simply words spoken, but rather they had the power to change situations and alter circumstances. Psalm 1:1 opens with a declarative blessing that has in its very essence what is promised to those who walk upright before the Lord. The Bible says, blessed are those who do not walk in the counsel of the ungodly, nor stand in the way of sinners, nor sit in the seat of the scornful. If you are to be in covenant relationship with the Father, you cannot be in relationship with the ungodly, nor stand in the way of sinners, nor sit in the seat of the scornful.

Jesus, in the Beatitudes, gives eight proclamations of blessings that clearly state who is blessed and why. To receive the blessings of the Lord, we must be meek, hunger and thirst for righteousness, be poor in spirit, pure of heart, merciful, be willing to be persecuted for Christ's sake and sometimes mourn. Are you willing to really live the Beatitudes so that you may see the blessing?

Now that we know, how God blesses us, let us examine how we bless Him. When He is the object of human blessing, the context is invariably one of worship and praise. When we bless God, we offer him praise for who He is and what he has done on behalf of those He loves. For example, Melchizedek blesses the God of Abraham for having delivered him from his enemies. Jethro, the Midianite priest, blesses Yahweh for having delivered the Israelites from Egypt. The women of Bethlehem praised God on Naomi's behalf for not leaving her without a descendant in the wake of her husband's death.

Have you, like the Biblical men and women blessed God lately? Or have you only sought His hand and not His face? Do you recognize Him as the all consuming fire, as the one who sustains and protects you? Do you bless Him because He not only created the heavens and the earth, but also because He rules and keeps them? Why not simply bless Him because He is God, He is immutable, without compare, almighty, everlasting, all knowing, and ever present. Oh, that we would bless Him because His name is excellent in all the earth and He is the Sovereign Lord. Why not bless Him because He alone is worthy of all praise, honor, worship and glory.

Man's version of being blessed is different than God's version. Scripture tells us in Lk 12:37(NLT): "Blessed are those servants whom the Master shall find on the alert waiting for His return; I tell you, that He will seat them Himself, put on an apron, and serve them, as they sit and eat. We must understand that being blessed has nothing to do with getting material things from God, but it has everything to do with our relationship with God.

References: KJV; NASB; Dictionary of the OT: Pentateuch

Scriptures: Gen: 25:11; Matt 5:3-11; Ps. 37:5; Gen 12:3; Dt. 7:14; Num 23:19; Dt. 28:1-14; Pr. 10:22

The Blood

Key Scripture: *For this is My Blood of the covenant, which is poured out for many for forgiveness of sins. ~Matt. 26:28*

Christ's blood redeems, cleanses, saves, and removes the sting of death. It symbolizes an unshakeable and unbreakable covenant with the Father. It covers and protects us while defeating the enemy. Deliverance, forgiveness and healing are found in the Blood. There is no atonement, reconciliation or remission of sin without it; for in both the Old and New Testaments blood was shed so that sinful man might be reconciled to a holy God. It is one of the strangest, deepest, mightiest, and most heavenly of God's thoughts. It is the very root of both the Old and New Covenants. Whereas the Old centered on the blood of beasts, the New is stamped with the precious Blood of the lamb.

Through the shedding of blood, Abraham became God's friend. Exodus 30:10 declares the Blood makes atonement for our souls. Isaiah resoundingly lets us know that the blood covers the crimson stain of sin and Genesis 4:10 tells us that the blood speaks. In 1 John we find that the Blood is a purifier.

The need of the Blood is to overcome the punishment for death. The Bible teaches that the soul that sins shall surely die and that the wages of sin is death. Therein lies the need for the Blood that we might have eternal life. In the blood is found the life of the flesh according to Lev. 17:11.

The meaning of the Blood is demonstrated in the Day of Atonement when the sacrifice was slain in the

36

outer court; the connotation being that death is an admittance of sin and guilt. The high priest then took the blood, entered into the most Holy place and sprinkled it on and near the Mercy Seat. This illustrates forgiveness and life and references to Christ's Blood. For Christ, the ultimate High Priest took His own Blood to the true mercy seat, into God's presence and presented it for the remission of all sins, of all believers, of all time.

The power of the Blood exemplifies the punishment of sin being removed. In its place we have spiritual, natural and eternal life. The Blood cleanses us from guilt through Christ's death. It releases us from sin's bondage through His resurrection and abolishes the enmity of sin by His ascension. We have been sanctified, justified, and made free by the Blood of the Lamb. Through Christ's shed blood on Calvary's cross sin, sickness, guilt, shame and death were defeated.

Pleading the Blood of Jesus is one of the most powerful weapons you can have in your arsenal as you wage war against the adversary. Because the devil is our accuser, the only successful plea is the Blood of Jesus. Simply put, to plead the Blood is to apply it to your life, much like Israel applied it to their doorposts. It is to take hold of the authority and power given to us through Christ's shed blood. The songwriter reminds us that the Blood still washes. The Blood still cleanses and after all these years, the Blood still has miraculous power.

References: NASB; The Two Covenants & the Second Blessing; The Essentials of Life

Scriptures: Gen 4:10, Ex 12:13-23; 30:10; Lev 14:5-7; 17:11; Ezek18:4; Matt 26:28; Act 20:28; Rom 3:25; 5:19; 1Cor 11:25; Eph 1:7; 2:13; Col 1:13-14; Heb 2:14; 9:22; 10:29; Rev; 12:11

Faith

Key Scripture: *For we walk by faith, not by sight. ~2 Cor 5:7*

Abraham is the model and father of faith. The Bible teaches us that we grow in faith. Without faith, we can't please God. We have etched 2 Cor. 5:7: for we walk by faith not by sight in our memory bank of well-known Scriptures. Jesus, in Matthew says that only a mustard seed's worth is needed to move the mountains in your life. Paul teaches in Ephesians that the shield of faith is part of our battle gear; while the writer of Hebrews speaks of the hall of faith and further states that Jesus is the author and finisher of our faith. Yet, true faith is often misunderstood and seldom exercised.

Faith is just as important in our secular lives. It is often seen in business deals where men are said to conduct business in good faith. We give good faith payments while broken contracts are called a breach of faith. Faith then is akin to the scarlet thread of redemption: you cannot live without it. That includes agreements we make with each other.

True faith must be present in all human relationships with man and the Father. Biblical faith is completely based on God's reliability and our response of trust in Him. Faith is essentially our belief in Jesus and the truth of His redemptive work on the Cross. Faith requires hope. For faith is the substance of things hoped for and the evidence of things not seen. Faith requires us to see in the spirit what is not there in the natural. Faith requires childlike dependence on the Lord and the total surrender of your will to God's will.

Faith is the lifeblood and foundation of the church. True faith is the opposite of intellectual knowledge. Real faith requires belief and trust in the God you have never seen or touched. It requires a personal commitment, often at a great cost. Israel operated in the belief that the God of Abraham, Isaac and Jacob, could and would deliver them even though they had never seen Him face to face. Conversely, intellectual knowledge requires no commitment or sacrifice. You need only have a temporal and fleeting belief in your abilities, talent, and sphere of influence.

Faith requires substance – both weight and wait (time). Things of substance are heavy and require effort to carry. Moses carried the weight of a people on his shoulders as he led them through the Promised Land. Through him, Israel developed faith in Jehovah. Faith is more than believing God for houses, cars, husbands and land. Faith believes Him for the eternal promises He has made. Faith perseveres when the very foundation of your soul is shaken to its core. Faith believes God even when you can't trace God. When the vicissitudes of life come, your level of faith will be evident and fully displayed.

How you handle valley experiences, signifies to God and the world whether you have learned to fully trust and depend on Him. Faith is a choice. What we choose says volumes about who we are. Just as we choose to trust God and have faith, on the flip side, we too often choose to get mired and bogged down in doubt, disbelief and despair.

How do I get faith you might ask? You cannot talk yourself into it; neither can you use human logic to rationalize or conceptualize it. Faith is simple: it is a matter of trust. It is asking God to help your unbelief. Faith is God's gift. He uses faith to purify our hearts and offers it to all who believe in Jesus. Remember faith is the key. It comes by hearing and following God's Word. With it, you can do all things through Christ who strengthens you. Without it, you will do little that matters in eternity. Do you trust and believe God enough to have faith in Him or will you walk in fear? Have you done as a favored hymn suggests: *Come this far by faith, leaning on the Lord?*

References: NASB, Boice Cmy; NLT Verse finder

Scriptures: Lev 6:2; Judges 9:15-16; Matt 17:20-22; Rom 3:22; Acts 15:9; 2 Tim 2:13; Jas 2:18-19; Heb 11:1-18; 12:1

Fasting

Key Scripture: *So we fasted and earnestly prayed that our God would take care of us and He heard our prayer. ~Ezra 8:23 (NLT)*

Fasting ushers you into God's presence. It brings you into a closer fellowship with Him. It is a secret source of power and connection to the Sovereign One. It will help you conquer the flesh and is often described as afflicting the soul. It is in essence sacrificing your personal will so that you may hear clearly from God and move forthwith.

Fasting can be done corporately or individually. There is no right or wrong amount of time one should give to fasting. Daniel mourned for 3 full weeks, whereas the Day of Atonement fast was 24 hours. The Savior instructs us to fast unto the Lord, not to impress men as the Pharisees did. Fasting allows us more time to pray, teaches us self-discipline, reminds us that we can live with far less than we think and most important, it helps us to appreciate God's gifts.

In the Old Testament, fasting was seen as a sign of repentance and was voluntary except for the Day of Atonement, which was mandated for all of Israel. Fasting should always be accompanied by prayer and time spent meditating on God's Word. Certainly you can fast without prayer; however when the two are combined with a sincere desire to touch the hem of His garment, the full effectiveness and power of the act is achieved. Dedicating a specific time to fast/pray is not meant to be a method of manipulating God into doing what we want. Rather, it is meant to bring you into a closer fellowship with Christ while crucifying your flesh.

Fasting forces you to focus and rely solely on God for strength, wisdom, and provision. Simply put, when you fast and pray your spirit is open to receive divine revelation from the Elohim God. As you earnestly seek the Almighty's presence through self-denial of food and/or liquids for a set period of time, you must activate your faith into believing that your Father in heaven will respond and His glory will fill your temple.

The Bible tells us that some deliverances will only come through fasting and prayer. Therefore, make fasting more than abstaining from food. Put your focus on the thoughts of God – what is His will and purpose for your life is, and what He wishes to say to you, do in you, with you and through you.

Fasting is not a fad diet or a weight management program. We would be wise to look to biblical examples found throughout Scripture for guidance on how and when to fast. Moses fasted 40 days before receiving the Decalogue. Samuel called for a national fast when Israel sinned. Elijah fasted 40 days before speaking with God. David fasted and prayed for his sick child. Anna worshipped day and night fasting and praying. Jesus fasted 40 days before Satan tempted him. The church at Antioch fasted and prayed before sending Paul and Barnabas out on their first missionary journey; they in turn, fasted before appointing church elders. What does this mean you ask? It means that fasting should be an integral part of any plan or serious move in your life as you seek God for answers.

How do I know if my fast is according to His will? Is what you're fasting and praying for bringing honor and glory to God? Is it found in Scripture? Is your flesh being satisfied or crucified? Finally, we must be mindful that if our fasting, praying, meditating and asking does not line up with God's will and His Word, we have done nothing more than engage in futile bodily exercise, which profits naught.

References: NASB; Smith's Bible Dictionary; Handbook of Bible Application

Scriptures: Ex 34:28; Lev. 23-32; Deut 9:9; 1 Sam 7:6; 2 Sam 12:16-17; 1Ki 19:8; 21: 9, 12; Ps 35:13; Isa 58:3; Dan. 10:2-3; Matt 4:2; 6:16-18; 17:20; Lk 2:37

Favor

Key Scripture: *For it is You who blesses the righteous man O, Lord, You surround him with favor as with a shield. ~Ps 5:12*

Favor is a popular topic of sermons and the subject of many beautiful melodies. It is defined as goodwill, acceptance, desire or pleasure from another. Children seek their parent's favor, just as adults often curry favor with men and women of great influence. We are told that the favor of God is greater than material wealth. But do we really know what favor is, how to get it, and what conditions are attached to it?

Favor is that level and place in God that goes above and beyond His blessings. In Scripture we find that God's favor is durable and without end. David declares God's anger is for a moment, but His favor is for a lifetime. Solomon teaches in the Book of Proverbs that we must first find wisdom if we are to obtain the Lord's favor. Mercy and truth must not forsake us, lest we forfeit the favor of both God and man. The Elohim God promises His favor to the righteous and to surround you with it as a shield.

How do we find this everlasting favor? When you revere the name of the Lord, He will favor you with His compassion. When the Father is pleased with you, His favor will fall fresh upon you, giving you unusual and divine ability. When God shines His face upon you, you may ask as the Psalmist did for God to remember you when He is granting favor to His people so that you will be among His chosen. Ask and it shall be given; seek and you shall find; knock and the door shall be opened. If it is favor you desire, seek it, ask for it and knock on Heaven's door to receive it.

Evidence that God's favor respects no particular person can be found in the history of these Biblical giants: in the midst of the flood, Noah found favor with God; in the midst of a famine, Joseph found favor with Pharaoh; in adversity, Ruth found favor with Boaz; in a seemingly lost cause, Gideon found favor in battle; as a young girl, Esther found favor with the King who the Bible says, loved her more than all the women in the land. Samuel found favor with God; David was favored as he sought a dwelling place for the tabernacle. Israel conquered her enemies because the favor of the Lord was with them. Mary, the mother of Jesus was favored to birth the Messiah, and Jesus, the Christ who grew in stature with God and men became the Savior to mankind.

Famed songwriter Donald Lawrence describes favor this way. He says: "God's favor can open the way, bring high places down, and turn things around. God's favor is more precious than life." When you truly come into the knowledge that God's favor is available to you, living with the confidence that He who began a good work in you will complete it until the day of Jesus Christ, will come more easily. You will dare to be bold. You will see enemies in a different light, understanding that you have the advantage because you sit in heavenly places with Christ Jesus. You really will walk with the expectation and belief that I cannot lose because I have the favor of God. You will look for the miracle, expect the impossible, feel the intangible and see the invisible. Thank you Clark Sisters.

Are you living favor-minded? Are you hoping to the end for the divine favor of God that is coming to you? Are you ready to proclaim this as the favorable year of the Lord in your life? We often obtain favor, not because of who we are or what we've done, we obtain favor because of who we know and our affiliation with them. For example, Joseph's brothers found favor in Pharaoh's sight because of Joseph. What they really deserved was death; instead, they were treated royally. Likewise, the same principle can be applied spiritually. We have no natural claim on God. However, He is favorable if we are sisters and brothers (joint heirs) of His Son, Jesus.

We all walk in God's blessings, but not everyone receives God's favor. Every breath you take and move you make is evidence of God's blessings. Jesse, David's father had 8 sons, all of whom were blessed; yet David, the youngest was favored. All of David's sons were blessed, but Solomon was favored. All the disciples were blessed to walk with Jesus, but James, John and Peter were favored. Prince Harry is blessed to be in England's royal family, but Prince William is favored, for he will one day be king.

So we ask, is this the favorable year of the Lord in your life? If the answer is no, I beseech you to seek the Father not just for His blessings, but for His favor which lasts a lifetime. The Father stands ready, knocking at your door; won't you let Him in?

References: CJB; NASB; Thompson Chain Topical Index

Scriptures: Gen 6:8; 12:3; 39:21; Ex 34:9; Judges 6:17; Ruth 2-4; 1 Sam 2:26; 2 Sam 15:25; 1Ki 3:10; 2Ki 13:14; Ps 5:12; 30:5; 90:17; 89:17; 147:11; Is 62:4; Zech 10:6; Lk 1:28, 30; 2:25; Acts 7:46; Eph 2:6; 1 Pet 1:13; Rev 3:20

Fire

Key Scripture: *The winds are Your messengers; flames of fire are Your servants. ~Ps 104:4 (NLT)*

It is mysterious, visible and warming. It cheers and comforts. It is at once terrible and consuming. It burns, purifies and guides. It is a representation of God's presence and the instrument of His power. Christians are believed to be baptized in it. It is used for sacrificial, domestic and war purposes. There is no nation, people or culture ever created that did not and does not continue to use fire in its everyday living.

Not only was fire used for heat, cooking, and as a method to make metal malleable, it was also used to dispose of contaminated clothing. Similarly, the Father uses the fire of the Holy Ghost to rid us of the contamination of the world so that we may become one of the holy people, serving a holy God who are clothed in His righteousness. Scripture says when we come into Christ, old things are passed away and all things have become new.

Fire was also one of the ways in which God revealed Himself or His will to Israel. It was what He used to call Moses to be the leader of His people through the burning bush and how he led and protected the children of Israel through their wilderness experience. Fire is illustrative of God's Word, the Holy Spirit, and the church overcoming her enemies.

It is metaphorically thought of as an example of the zeal of saints (on fire for the Lord), angels (a flaming fire), man's wickedness (those condemned to hell will be in the lake of fire that is never satisfied).

Symbolically, fire is spoken of as a purifying element, an emblem of healing and as part of Israel's covenant with God. Used sacredly, fire consumed the burnt offering, the incense offering, and burned on the altar of God without ever being extinguished. It was through fire that God showed Himself to Isaiah, Ezekiel, and the apostle John and it is by fire that He will appear at His second coming.

God is compared to fire not only because of His glorious and incomparable brightness, but also on account of His anger against sin. The Word tells us the fire of God consumes sinners. Fire also manifests as an example of God's abiding love and concern for His children. Through fire, He tested the faithful, protected Elisha, carried Elijah to heaven and showed His perpetual presence with Israel. The Father uses fire to purge, purify and cleanse.

In the New Testament, Luke likened the outpouring of the Holy Spirit in Acts as tongues of fire. Paul tells us in Corinthians that our very foundation will be tested by fire in order to reveal the endurance of our faith. The Holy Spirit will cleanse, search, illuminate, refine and purify by fire. He burns up the dross in our lives when we allow Him to enter and take possession of our hearts. It is also by fire that God will judge the wicked. Matthew clearly states that the godless will be as chaff, burned with an unquenchable fire.

Often we sing let the fire of the Holy Ghost fall on me, but do we mean that? What would happen if the fire of the Holy Ghost really fell on you? Are you willing to live with the changes that happen after God's fire and anointing hit you? Having the fire of God fall on you will require a lifestyle shift, a renewing of your talk and your walk as well as a transforming of your mind

To do the work of God effectively and to be His witness, we need to be immersed in fire. Sadly, it is possible to say we are baptized with the Holy Spirit but not have a spark plug worth of fire. As believers, we have attended seminars and conferences that have not affected us, let alone the world. What we need now is a fresh filling of Holy fire so that we can demonstrate the power of God to a hungry and dying world. For Matthew 3:11-12 says John the Baptist baptized with water, but Jesus baptized with both the Holy Ghost and fire.

The Lord has promised to be a protective wall of fire around you. Jesus is seen as a refiner's fire and the Word is said to be like a fire that can break a rock into pieces. Is the Word of the Lord burning in you? Is His Spirit upon you like fire? Have you been tried in the fire and found to be as silver and gold refined? If not, won't you let the fire of God make you, mold you, shape you, and prepare you to be used for His glory and in His Kingdom?

References: CJB; NASB; Eerdman's Bible Dictionary; Great Doctrines of the Bible; Renn's Expositional Dictionary; Smith's Bible Dictionary; New Topical Dictionary

Scriptures: Gen 8:20; 15:17; Ex 3:2; 32:24; 40:13; Lev 13: 52, 57; Dt 5:24-26; 32:22; 2 Ki 2:11; 6:17; Ps 39:3; 104;4; Isa 4:5-6; 6:4; 9:18; Jer 5:14; 23:29; Eze 1:4-5; Oba 1:18; Zech 2:5; Mal 3:2-3; 4:1; Matt 3:12;13:42; Lk 3:16; Acts 2:3-4; 2 Thess 1:7; Rev 1:12-14

Friend

Key Scripture: *There is no greater love than to lay down one's life for one's friend. ~Jn 15:15 (NLT)*

We have friendly churches, user-friendly machines and friendship evangelism. Often behind the rhetoric is a deep craving for what is seldom experienced – intimate, lifelong relationships in which persons are enjoyed simply for who they are and not for what they can do for us. Ironically, people who boast of having an abundance of friends may be among the loneliest people we know. Yet to contrast loneliness and embrace true friendships, we need look no further than the Bible.

Christ makes it very plain that both He and the Father desire a very special type of relationship with true believers (Rev 3:20). He tells us that He stands at the door, knocking, waiting for us to let Him in. When you are alone, as we all really are, you need something – indeed, someone. In fact, what you desperately need is precisely what God wants to provide for you – A FRIEND!

Even though we often have personal relationships with people that are not always intimates, we only tell our deep secrets and most heartfelt dreams to those whom we cherish the most and call friend. The friendship we have with Jesus is absolutely amazing and beyond anything we could ever have hoped for, especially when we realize that He is not only the Son of God, but the Savior of the World. However, Jesus longs to have a bond with us that is at once personal and intimate.

At times it's overwhelming to grasp the truth of what it means is to be a friend of Jesus Christ. True friendship with the Savior takes us to the center of Christian living and assures us in the presence of the Elohim God.

As much as we easily relate to being a child of God or a servant of God, the Father desires more – He wants us to be His friend!

If we are going to be a friend of God and therefore a friend to man, there are a few rules we must adhere to. We must recognize that:

Real friendship involves loyalty. What kind of friend are you? There is a vast difference between being acquainted with someone and really knowing them as a true friend. The greatest evidence of genuine friendship is loyalty. God was a loyal friend to Moses even when Moses wasn't friendly. Solomon says a friend will stick closer than a brother; will make you better and will lift you up when you fall.

On the other hand, we must also be aware of false friends, even in the church. There are few hurts as deep as those from your Christian brothers/sisters (e.g. Delilah was not Samson's friend; likewise, David was not Uriah's friend).

Speaking of disloyalty, we all know that Judas was not Jesus' friend. Even His trusted disciple Peter denied Him. When we look at betrayal of friends, especially those in the church, we can become bitter and hardhearted. However, we must remember the lyrics of an old church hymn, what a friend we have in

Jesus, all our sins and grieves to bear, what a privilege to carry everything to God in prayer.

Isn't it wonderful to know we don't have to carry our hurts and pains? Jesus assures us in Luke that "no one who has left home, a wife, or brother, or parents, or children for the sake of the kingdom of God [30] will fail to receive many times as much in this age and, in the age to come, eternal life."

To that end, please know that real friendship is found with Jesus. Because Jesus Christ is Lord and Master, He should call us servants; instead He calls us friends. He laid down His life for His friends (do you have a friend you're really willing to die for)? What are you willing to give up and let go of because of your Friend?

Greater love has no man than this that a man lay down his life for his friends. Real friendship is imitating Christ in our relationships. As much as Jesus calls us His friend, we must be mindful that we are not His equal. As such, we must always approach Him with reverence, respect and honor that is due His name. Just as we know that Christ is our friend, we must take care to be His friend. We can take comfort in our friendship with Jesus because we are His beloved. Additionally, the benefit of the relationship is rooted in the characteristics, the comfort and the conditions.

>   a.   The Characteristics of Friendship with Jesus will include: The fruit we bear and the fact we are called sons and children of God;

b.   The Comfort in our friendship with Jesus comes because we are his beloved; and

c.   The Condition of our friendship with Jesus means we must be obedient, keep His commands and be born of God.

Once we have the characteristics, comfort and condition of our friendship with Christ in order, only then can we recognize that our very effectiveness is directly proportional to our INTIMACY with our heavenly Father and his Son, Jesus Christ. When God inspired Isaiah to write those famous, oft-quoted words: "Come now, let us reason together" (Isaiah 1:18). He was essentially extending an open invitation to each of us to get to know Him, not just as our Father or Creator or Master, but as our friend. Those individuals who throughout history have been the most effective in interceding with God have been his friends – not those who have been casually acquainted with Him.

Friendship with the Father must contain these four elements: commitment, companionship, communication and compassion. If we are to be friends of God, we must first be committed. Secondly, we must become committed companions. Third, our committed companionship must lead to honest and fervent communication. That means we are to listen to our Friend more than we talk. Finally, as committed companions in constant communication, we must have compassion for God's people. We must love others as Christ loves us and do unto others as we would have them do unto us.

There is no greater act of compassion than one man laying down His life for another. It is the price Jesus paid for our sins – He hung on a cross. What will you lay down for your friend? Will you be as Esther and risk death? She recognized that her life was to be used as a gift for her friends and family as a result a people were saved from destruction.

A wise old saint once said you must be a friend to the one you seek to win. We admonish you to let Jesus be your perfect example. He was a friend to the lost, the lame, the unloved, the sick, the diseased, and the distressed; yet the songwriter says, there's not a friend like the lowly Jesus, no not one, no not one.

References: NASB; CJB; Boice Cmy; Renn's Expositional Dictionary; Smith Bible Dictionary

Scriptures: Gen 18:7; 26:12-16; Ex 33:11; Ruth 1:16-18; 1 Sam 18:1; Psa 55:12-14; Pro 13:20; 17:17; 18:24; Eccl 2:2-10; Jer 3:4; Matt 11:19; Lk 19:7; Jn 15:13-17; Jas 2:23

Gift

> **Key Scripture:** *Every good thing given and every perfect gift is from above, coming down from the Father of lights. ~ (Jas 1:17)*

Most of us eagerly anticipate receiving gifts and many of us find great joy in giving them. Children inform their parent's months in advance of their birthday what they would like to have as one. Spouses dare not forget them on special days. We give gifts to celebrate, to say thanks or simply just because. Some are expensive, some not so much. Many gifts are handmade with lots of love and attention, while others are hastily put together as an afterthought. Some come with strings attached; while others are freely given. Yet we could never give or receive a gift as precious as what God has given us. He gave His only begotten son Jesus that we might have eternal life.

You can be given everything imaginable to man, but unless the person gives you themselves, there is still emptiness. It is how God feels when we only give a portion of ourselves to Him and save the best for the world. We spend ten minutes in prayer, three hours in the mall, and endless hours cheering for our beloved sports team or mindlessly doing nothing and wondering where the time went. We turn off the phone and shut out the family to watch an hour long TV program, yet we give God 15 minutes of Bible study.

We do God a favor and attend Sunday worship services while the other six days we "do our own thing." What would become of us if God treated us in the same cavalier manner? Your gift to God is as a thermometer of your soul. It reveals what you think, if you can give or whether you can truly love. We must give God our very best, not what's leftover. Never forget, He gave His best.

Sadly, there are those who will refuse the Gift and all that He offers. To those, Scripture teaches that the wages of sin is death. Will you choose death or life, sin or God, wages or His free gift? Remember, wages are earned (sin); gifts are freely given (salvation). We must decide if we will live in eternity with the gift Giver or with the one who comes to kill, steal and destroy.

Not only has the Father given us eternal gifts, He has given us spiritual gifts. Just as there is a difference in the blessings God gave to each tribe, there is also a difference in gifts given to each person. There are varieties of gifts; but the same Spirit. Likewise, there are varieties of ministries, but the same Lord. Some have the motivational gifts. Others are equipped with the manifestation gifts, while many have the ministry gifts. No matter what area you are gifted in, please know your gift is valuable to the body of Christ. You must also recognize that no one gift is more important than another. Gifts given by the Father are both a divine blessing and a measure of God's grace and love for us.

We must never envy another person's gifts, instead look at the gifts God has given you and resolve to do what He has uniquely qualified you to do. If we are wise we will seek to worship Him as we use our gifts. Understand that spiritual gifts were never given to glorify flesh; rather they were given that we might accomplish His good works according to His will. We are given gifts to unite, build up and equip the church for service in the Lord's Kingdom. Fully accepting God's greatest gift for who He is will ensure that as you operate in the gifts of the Spirit, you will first walk in the fruit of the Spirit. We say thanks be to God for His indescribable, irreplaceable and immutable gift – Jesus Christ, Savior of the world.

References: NASB; Boice Cmy; Everyday Christianity Handbook; Smith Bible Dictionary

Scriptures: Gen 33:11; Nu 18:6-7; Judges 14:20; 1 Sam 10:27; Esther 9:19, 22; Prov 18:16; 19:6; Jn 3:16; Rom 6:23; 12: 6-8; 1 Cor 12: 4-10; Eph 4:11; Heb 11:4

God

Key Scripture: *God said I AM that I AM. I am the LORD. ~(Ex 3:14; 6:2)*

He is the Supreme Being, the Creator and Ruler of the universe. We all believe in a God; yet not everyone believes in or knows the true and living God. Questions remain. Who is God? From where did He come? The answer: He did not come from anywhere, He always has been and He shall always be. His existence is taken for granted by millions. Many more would argue that the Bible doesn't provide proof that God is. Yet Psalm 14:1 calls those who do not believe in Him fools. Even though we have never seen or touched Him, we have the Word as our guide. In it we find that God is a Spirit, and they that worship Him do so in spirit and truth.

The Creator is known by many names: Lord, Jehovah, Elohim, Father, or God. As the Sovereign One, He is a multiplicity of things all at once. He is the creator and sustainer of the universe. He is God the Son who gave His life that we may live. He is God the Holy Spirit, the advocate, teacher, and comforter who endues us with power. The Bible declares He has no beginning or ending.

Jehovah God is the great I AM. His nature and being are infinite. His essence is immutable. He is the same today, yesterday and forevermore. He need only take counsel with Himself. God simply "IS."

He is the El Shaddai, almighty, omnipotent God. His voice causes the earth to quake and the heavens to declare His glory. The Psalmist proclaims that His law is perfect, converts the soul and makes wise the simple. The LORD is full of majesty. His breath gives life and His wrath can bring death. He is God and beside Him there is no other. God simply "IS."

God is Elohim, the self-existing one who neither sleeps nor slumbers. He is sovereign and supreme. He is subject to and influenced by none. God's plan cannot be thwarted or hindered. He is the God of all flesh and nothing is too hard for Him. God sits in the heavens and whatever He pleases comes to pass. He is the potter and we are His clay – molded and shaped according to His foreknowledge and predestination. God simply "IS."

God is holy, perfect and pure. He is light and no darkness is within Him. Arthur Pink says the sum of all moral Excellency is found in Him. We thank Him because He is faithful, never forgets or fails. We bless Him because He is love. He doesn't just love; He is love. We honor Him because He is King of kings. We magnify His name because His goodness and mercy pursues us forever. We glorify Him because at His right hand are pleasures forevermore. God simply "IS."

God is omnipresent, everywhere at all times. He is outside of time, space and human limitations. He is whatever you need Him to be. He is joy, comfort, refuge and strength. God is Raphe the healer, Shalom your peace; Tsidkenu the righteous one; Nissi, your banner, the God who fights for you. He is Jireh the one who provides and Rohi, the Shepherd who cares for you. He is Alpha & Omega. He is eternal, from everlasting to everlasting and throughout all generations. To encapsulate the fullness and plurality of God we quote an old church mother who simply said, "GOD ARE" all that you will ever need!

References: NASB; The Attributes of God

Scriptures: Gen 2:7; Ex 3:14; 6:2; Ps 19:1, 7; 115:3; Isa 45:18; 48:16; 64:8; Jer 29:11; 32:27; Jn 4:25; Eph 1:1; 1 Thess 1:19; Heb 13:8; Jas 1:17; 1 Jn 1:5; Rev 15:4

Heart

Key Scripture: *Glory in His holy name; let the heart of those who seek the LORD be glad ~1 Chr 16:10*

The heart can be filled with love or with hate. Many are courageous; some are fearful. The Bible says the heart can overflow with gladness or be consumed by sadness. It is the seat of man's will and becomes the source of good and evil behavior. The heart is the center of bodily life and is the reservoir of the entire life-power. The heart is the deepest place where the attributes of man's personality are found.

Only God, through His grace can transform and renew your heart. The process of heart renewal is indicated in Scripture in various ways. A stony heart is removed, and is only fixed through fearing God; it becomes clean and with it man believes in the Savior. It is in one's heart where the Spirit of the Son is found and God's love is poured forth. Yet, the same God, from His judgment seat can harden your enemy's heart.

The Bible clearly outlines what is good and bad about the condition of the heart. A bribe will corrupt the heart; deceit is found therein; sin is committed there; and a fool will say there is no God. Conversely, Scripture says a joyful heart is good and they that are pure in heart are blessed of God. Understand, what you think in your head, your heart becomes. Where your treasure is, the desires of your heart will be also. It is the heart that determines the depth of your relationship with the Father, for your heart is the focal point of His dealings with you.

70

Found in our heart is the response to God's revelation, for it bears witness to the existence of both our heart and our connection to His Sovereignty. It is how we become responsible for our own thinking, acting and willing. We are commanded to love the Lord with all our heart, soul and mind. Jesus in the book of John admonishes us to not allow our hearts to be troubled, for we are to believe in both the Father and the Son. The result is a strengthening of our hearts.

In Scripture, the "heart" always takes precedence, because lodged within it are the innermost hidden things. In our hearts we hide the Word. In our hearts we process self-consciousness. In our hearts we presume and determine to do a thing – good or bad. In our hearts we find the connection to the psychological or religious state of our mind. In our hearts sits the very core of who we are and who we will become.

In both the Old and New Testaments God's love is based in the heart. The Father has so designed us that our heart is the center of the feelings and affections of joy, pain, despair, fear, reverential trembling, praise and worship.

Have you examined what is in your heart lately?

Do you love Him with the entirety of your being? Remember, it is simply a matter of the heart.

References: NASB; NLT; Eerdman's Bible Dictionary; ISBE; New Unger's Bible Dictionary; NASB Topics

Scriptures: Ex 4:21; Lev 19:17; Dt 8:14; 13:3; 2 Sam 17:10; Neh 2:2; Ps 14:1;

71

51:10; 119:11; Prov 6:18; 11:20; 12:20; 23:7; 27:11; Eccl 7:7; Is 35:4; Eze 1:19; Matt 5:8, 28; 6:21; Lk 10:27; Rom 5:5; 10:10; Gal 4:6; Phil 4:7

Heaven

Key Scripture: *Forever, O LORD, Your word is settled in heaven. ~Ps 119:89*

We sing about heaven. It is the premise and foundation on which most houses of worship are built. We envision what heaven looks like, who will be there and what we will do once we arrive. Artists have drawn, painted, carved and sculpted priceless works depicting how they believe God's throne room will appear. Yet even in our most vivid imagination, the size, the scope, the glory, the splendor and majesty of heaven is far beyond what we could ever conceive. Heaven is the eternal resting place Christians long to see, touch and ultimately inhabit.

It is the divine creation and possession of God. Heaven is not limited to or constrained by the boundaries of space or time. It is not confined to one location; Isaiah says that God inhabits eternity. As such His dwelling place is not subject to our miniscule thoughts or finite dimensions.

Folklore says Peter is standing at the gates of heaven deciding who enters. Is he really? Do we believe that the Father would leave it up to Peter, one who was brought forth in iniquity and conceived in sin just as we were to decide who enters into the eternal Kingdom? Hardly! However, many have questions about who will dwell on God's holy hill. The answer is simple and clearly depicted in the Bible. Psalm 15:1-5 says we must walk in integrity, work righteousness, speak truth, never slander, do no evil, and honor and fear the Lord, among other things. That means your entry into your eternal inheritance cannot be dependent on the prayers of your righteous relatives.

Because each of us must see Jesus face to face, it is incumbent upon us that we live a holy and pleasing life before the Lord.   Remember, God has no grandchildren, only children.

Where is heaven you might ask? It is the place where our hope, our treasure, our inheritance and our name shall be found. Heaven is the place Jesus went to prepare for us. John, in Revelation 5, says "it is the place where God sits upon His throne, where the angels, elders, and a host engage in singing the praises of the Lamb. It is a lively place, with harps and bowls of fragrant incense, mansions and streets of gold." The Bible declares that God's habitation is the highest of the heavens. The heaven we long for is up above the atmospheric and starry heavens.

Heaven is the place from which God displays His unending love, where He metes judgment and executes wrath. Matthew 7:13 "says many will go through the wide gate of destruction; few will enter the narrow gates of life." We admonish you to choose you this day who you will serve. Your resting place in eternity is predicated on the choice you make. To quote a sacred hymn, Oh, I want to see Him, look upon His face; there to sing forever of His saving grace. On the streets of glory let me lift my voice; cares all past, home at last, ever to rejoice. Live so heaven will someday be your home.

References: NASB; AMG's Encyclopedia of Bible Facts; Boice Cmy; Expository Dictionary of Bible Words; Great Doctrines of the Bible; Smith's Bible Dictionary

Scriptures: Gen 1:1; Ex 20:11; Dt 26:15; Ps 15:1-5; Eccl 5:12; Isa 57:15; Matt. 5:7-12, 17-20; 7:13-14; Mk 10:21; Lk 10:20; 20:4; Jn 14:2; Col. 1:5; 3:1-5; 1 Pet 1:4; 2 Pet 3:13; Rev 21:10-16

Holiness

Key Scripture: *Follow peace with all men, and holiness, without which no man shall see the Lord. ~Heb 12:14*

Holiness is the characteristic of God most mentioned in the Bible. Without it no man can see Jesus. It belongs to God and to those who have been consecrated to His service. The Ark symbolized it and the Father demands it. Holiness should be a serious pursuit of anyone who is called a Christian.

Holiness is a lifestyle. It is not a denomination. To be holy is to be in the image according to the likeness of God our Father. Are we ever as holy as the Lord? In a word – no. Can we live a life of holiness that is pleasing to Him? The short answer is yes, we can and yes we must. Why, you might ask? Because Scripture tells that we must be holy; for the Lord our God is holy.

Christian joy and holiness depends almost entirely upon how well we know God's truth; that is, how well we know and practice the principles of God's written revelation. To illustrate this, Jesus began His discourse in John 17 by emphasizing both joy and holiness. God does not ask for 50 percent of who or what we are. He wants 100%. As a line from a famous gospel hymn says 99.5% won't do. Yes, to be partially holy, is to be completely carnal.

You can't mix oil and water neither can you mix holiness and sin. God wants all of us, and He insists on genuine holiness. Yet, in our efforts to become holy vessels, fit to be used by God for His glory and in His kingdom, we must remember that we cannot serve

God and man too. Holiness is the Lord's demand, not His request.

For many Christian's today, holiness is not in the forefront of their thoughts. Many hardly know what it means, which explains why we so seldom look for it in others. Far too often search committees make holiness low on the totem pole of characteristics they look for in new pastors or church leaders. Rather they want someone who is charismatic, communicates well and who has excellent administrative skills. While all those things are important, we must first find and fulfill God's emphasis on holiness, knowing that one day "Holy to the Lord" will be inscribed on us and we will be the Lord's holy people forever sitting at the right hand of the Father as a joint heir with Christ.

In the highest sense holiness belongs to God and to those He calls His own. We must realize that personal holiness is a work of measured development. Unfortunately, through carnality, fear, sin and worldliness, it is often hindered, hence the frequent commands throughout Scripture to be watchful, to pray, and to persevere. Understand that, praying, fasting and persevering alone will not ensure we become holy vessels. Holiness can only come from God. Holiness can only come from knowing His Word and allowing that Word to hide in your heart.

Whereas joy is the mark of the Christian in relationship to himself; holiness is the mark in our relationship to God. The immutable God does not change. His standard of holiness and righteousness is the same yesterday, today and forevermore. We must remember that in the end, the Lord is more concerned with your holiness than He is with your happiness. A songwriter says it best: I call you holy Lord you are holy You are so holy to me! I call you holy, Lord you are holy, holy you are and holy you'll be.

References: NASB; Boice Cmy; NASB Topics

Scriptures: Lev. 19:2; Ps 119:11; Isa 6:3; Mal 4:4; Jn 15:4; 17:17-19; Rom 6:19, 22; 1 Cor 1:30; 2 Cor 7:1; Eph 1:4; Titus 1:8; Heb 12:14; Rev 4:8; 15:4

Holy Spirit

> **Key Scripture:** *Now may the God of hope fill you with all joy and peace in believing, so that you will abound in hope by the power of the Holy Spirit. ~Rom 15:13*

He is identified with the Father and the Son. Personal acts and characteristics are ascribed to Him. His name is divine, as are both His works and attributes. To resist, insult, grieve, lie to, quench or blaspheme Him is to insult Him. The unconverted can't bear to hear of Him. There are even ministers who do not like to preach of Him. Many simply do not understand Him, while others refuse to accept Him.

His office work is to convict of sin, impart the love of God, fill us with hope and courage, give us liberty to testify of Christ, teach us all things, guide us into all truth and convert us. He is the Holy Spirit of the living God.

Many question if the Holy Spirit has a personality. For them acts of the Spirit are seen as mystical and secret. The visible creation makes the personality of the Father easy to conceive and the incarnation of the Son impossible to disbelieve. So much is said of His influence, grace, power, and gifts until we overlook the fact that He is more than an influence, power or manifestation of divine nature; He is a Person – the third Person of the Trinity who has been since the beginning of time and will be throughout all eternity.

He is called by many names. He is breath, wind, and power. He is the Comforter. He is the Spirit of Truth and the Spirit of Life. He is the Spirit of God and of Christ. Symbols used to describe Him are oil, fire, water, and the dove. Do not assume these names or symbols mean He is nothing more than an impersonal authority that emanates from God. To do so would deny His divinity.

His attributes are divine: He is omnipresent, omnipotent, omniscient and eternal in His nature. His workings are from heaven above; He is seen in creation, salvation, and the resurrection. He edifies the church and He testifies of Christ, the risen Savior. Entry into God's kingdom can only come through the regenerating unction and power of the Holy Spirit.

Should you ever be in doubt about who He is or what place He has in your life, know this: the Holy Spirit empowers you to be a witness for Christ. He lives in and sanctifies you. He opens your spiritual eyes. Through Him you are born again. He makes intercession for you when you don't know what to pray. He was given by the Father as a comforter. His indwelling makes your body His temple. When He operates in your heart, He will give you power and fill you with wisdom and knowledge.

If ever you need guidance as to what, how, when, where and why, just seek out the Holy Spirit. He is there ready to direct, instruct and guide. When you feel alone, remember God has sent you a teacher and helper. When you feel conviction, it is He who is at work. If it is courage and strength you need, just call Him. He is an answer to prayer. If a change in conversation is what you seek, call Him for He is able to give you a new language and fill you with His grace. If power is what you seek, call on Him for the Father has promised to pour out His Spirit upon you. If an understanding of the Word is what you need, just call Him. He will interpret Scripture in such a way, that you will clearly hear the voice of God. If you allow Him, He will seal you, fill you, empower you, guide you, chasten you and anoint you. He is the Holy Spirit of the living God.

References: NASB; Great Doctrines of the Bible; NLT Verse Finder; Treasury of Great Preaching

Scriptures: Gen 1:2; Neh 9:20; Job 33:4; Ps 104:30; Prov 1:23; Isa 11:2; 61:1-2; Mic 3:8; Zec 4:6; Lk 4:18; 11:13; Jn 3:5-8;14:16;15:26; 16:13,17; Acts 5:9; 7:51; 9:31; Rom 8:2, 11; 26; 1 Cor 2:14; 3:16; 6:19; Eph 4:30; Tit 3:5; 1 Jn 5:6

Honor

Key Scripture: *Be devoted to one another in brotherly love; giving preference to one another in honor. ~Rom 12:10*

Honor means to be counted and treated as holy; to be sanctified and set apart. It means to be esteemed, made distinctive, distinguished and different. It is often mentioned in the recognition of one's service or rank. It can also refer to the price or value of a person or thing. It is the fifth of the Ten Commandments. The Bible says it is an inheritance. Honor—man desires it; God demands it.

In the Old Testament, knowing whom to honor and how to act in ways that would be considered honorable were critical if you were to successfully navigate life in Israel. The fate of Israel, the people whom God called by His name was ultimately tied into their honor of the Lord. Connection with the Name was Israel's connection with Jehovah's blessing and honor. In Numbers 6:23-27, we see that the placement of God's name upon Israel led to her blessings.

The Bible admonishes us to be vessels of honor, fit to be used for the Master's glory in His Kingdom. The godly show honor and respect with compassion, generosity of spirit and with righteousness of heart and mind. We are to honor the Son as we give honor to the Father. We are to honor and respect our parents. Men are to prize and exalt their wives. In return she will esteem and honor you. I Tim 5:3 tells us to honor the widows, while Peter encourages us to honor all people, love the brotherhood and fear God.

We are commanded to honor the Lord by studying his Word that we may come to know him. We honor God by trusting Him through life's trials and disappointments. We honor the Lord by praising Him as the source of all good. We give honor to God with our wealth by paying tithes and offerings, with the fruit of our lips and by speaking well of Him through our praise and worship. We honor the King by using our gifts and talents for His glory and the up building of the Kingdom. We honor Him by living holy, through our reverence and by keeping away from strife.

Yet some, who through disobedience, rebellion and stubbornness fall into dishonor. They willfully choose to deny the existence and power of God. But the Bible says that those who choose to show contempt for God by neglecting and violating His commandments, laws, precepts, and statutes subject themselves to God's judgment, anger, rebuke, or wrath.

Your duty to honor the Father, Son and Holy Spirit is based on divine revelation and not natural law. All true honor comes from God; all other honor is meaningless and passing. It's easy to honor one's self. You can, with no problems surround yourself with a false glory. It is simple enough – in fact, it is fatally easy – to bask in the glory of your own wonderfulness. Likewise, it is not overly difficult to win honor from men. The world honors the successful and the ambitious. But the real honor is the honor which only eternity can reveal. We must always put the calling of God above the honors of men. This day, choose whom you will serve because the God of your Salvation deserves all glory and honor.

References: NASB; Boice Cmy; PWS NT;
Dictionary of the Old Testament:
Pentateuch; Handbook of Bible
Application

Scriptures: Ex 7:5; 10:2; 14:4, 17-18;
20:12; Nu 6:23-27; Ezra 7:11-28; Prov 4:
8; 8:18; 12:9; 15:33; 20:3; Mal 3:10; Matt
15:8; Jn 5:23, 49; 12:26; Eph 6:2

Jesus

Key Scripture: *Jesus said, I am the way, and the truth, and the life; no one comes to the Father but through Me. ~Jn 14:6*

Some only know His name. Others have experienced His power. He grants grace and mercy to millions the world over. Nations have been saved by His Blood. And the world awaits His imminent and glorious return.

Some know Him as the Lion of Judah. Others call Him master. Many recognize Him as the Chief Shepherd. The prophets spoke of Him. All things came into being through Him. He is the Bread of Life and the bright and Morning Star. He is the Beloved and only begotten Son. He is the True Vine. He is Rabboni, the Way, the Truth and the Life. He is the good Shepherd. He is the Creator and Sustainer of all life. He is the Logos and the Beginning of all things.

He came to do the will of the Father and that you might have abundant life. He came to serve. He came for the remission of our sins. He came in the fullness of time. He possesses all power and authority. He came to fulfill the Law and to testify of the truth. He came to destroy the works of the devil. His name is Wonderful Counselor, Prince of Peace, Emmanuel, Son of David, Lamb of God, and Redeemer.

His Blood is powerful and cleanses your conscience from dead works. His Blood causes you to overcome, frees you from sin, and gives you eternal life. At His name, demons will tremble and flee. At His name every knee will bow and tongue will confess that He is Lord.

90

He bore all sin, sickness and disease on the cross. He died that you might live. He was without sin. His present ministry is carried out in heaven where He represents the saints before the throne of God. He is the eternal Son of God, clothed with human nature to bring salvation to man. His name signifies Savior. His title signifies anointed. He was born of a virgin. The government was upon His shoulders. He is the wisdom and power of God unto salvation.

He was anointed of God as the Prophet, Priest, and King. He is God come in the flesh. Of whom do we speak? Jesus!

References: CJB; NASB; The New Unger's Bible Dictionary, Eerdman's Bible Dictionary; ISBE

Scriptures: Gen 4:4; Matt 5:17; 18:11; Jn 3:17; 6:25-27; 32-35; 53:57; 10:10; Gal 4:4; 1 Tim 1:15; Heb 9:13-14; 1 Jn 2:1; 10:11; Rev 1:5-6

Joy

Key Scripture: *In Your presence is fullness of joy; in Your right hand there are pleasures forever. ~Ps 16:11*

Joy is an unspeakable, untouchable, and intangible feeling that we all long for and earnestly seek. In God's presence, its fullness is manifested. The songwriter says, the world didn't give it to us and the world can't take it away. Joy is often associated with happiness, but the two are very different. Happiness is based on the external, whereas joy is intrinsically connected to our divine relationship with the Father. Happiness depends on outside circumstances: a new dress, a new car, a house, a blossoming relationship or dream vacation. Joy on the other hand, comes from God and is present in spite of persecution, trials or adverse situations.

Joy is defined as a great feeling, as delight or pleasure. These words only define the expression of a wonderful emotion. What they do not describe are the causes of or circumstances in which joy is expressed. Joy is one of the nine Fruit of the Spirit wherein we must operate before we exercise the Gifts of the Spirit. True joy is evident regardless of the test. Most assuredly, neither Paul nor Silas was happy with their imprisonment, yet their fervent, joyful prayer and praise prompted the Father to cause an earthquake, resulting in their supernatural deliverance. True joy abounds even in the most distressing times and will cause us to offer a sacrifice of praise.

Joy is eternal and is found at the altar of God. Joy increases in the midst of struggle. True joy requires suffering. Even in our darkest hour, we can count on joy when encountering various trials because we are assured that the Savior in heaven has a greater reward awaiting us. The Bible says the godly sing for joy because the Lord has promised to turn your mourning into joy and give you joy for sorrow. Psalm 30:5 promises that joy will come in the morning. Isaiah suggests that the oil of joy can be applied to those who mourn. It is established in the joy of the Lord wherein you receive strength.

Happiness is contingent on a feeling and is temporal. Happiness and unhappiness will never coexist together. Yet sorrow and grief can and often do rest side by side. Jesus was described as a man of sorrows, acquainted with grief...but for the joy set before Him, endured the cross.

Triumphant joy through Christ Jesus is the predominant theme of the entire book of Philippians. In it, Paul expresses joy during his time of affliction and uncertain future. True joy requires you to remain in the Father's love and keep His commandments that your joy may be complete. True joy is equated with righteousness and peace in and through the Holy Spirit. True joy is dynamic and not static; it is available through worship of the only One who can present you faultless in His presence with great joy.

Are you living a life filled with eternal and everlasting joy or is your cup overflowing with the temporal and replaceable trappings of happiness? Jesus is waiting to be the center of your joy.

References: NASB; NKJ; IVP Dictionary of the New Testament

Scriptures: Neh 8:10; Ps 16:11; 30:5;
132:9; Is 53:3; Jer 1:16; 31:13; Acts
16:25-29; Heb 12:2; Jas 1:2; Jude 24

Justification

Key Scripture: *Therefore, having been justified by faith, we have peace with God through our Lord Jesus Christ. ~Rom 5:1*

Sin, transgression, and iniquity; we've all committed at least one of them. Fear, guilt, and shame; we've all felt them. But thanks be unto God there is hope. We have been justified and freed by His grace through the redemption found in Jesus Christ. Our sins are now covered under the powerful Blood of the Lamb.

Justification is a judicial act of God, whereby He declares us to be free from guilt and the consequences of sin. As justified believers, we have been acquitted and vindicated by God and brought into a right and faithful relationship with Him. It is through our faith in Christ that we are made free. At Calvary, Jesus bore all sins that we may be found without spot or wrinkle.

Scripture shows that justification involves three basic essentials:

a.   Remission of punishment – is not just a pardon; but a declaration that we are not guilty;

b.   Restoration to favor – we are entreated as though we have never sinned; and

c.   New legal standing before God – we are no longer under sin's condemnation because the Savior took our place when He hung on the cross.

Therefore, walking in guilt and shame serves no purpose. If we have been justified by faith, why do we insult the Father by reclaiming what Christ overcame on the cross? A songwriter put it this way: In God's chemical laboratory of redemption, He took my black soul, dipped it in red blood and it came out white as snow. Never allow others to remember what God has chosen to forget? What have you done, said or thought that is not covered under the Blood? The Father loves us so much that "He gave His only begotten Son that whoever believes in Him shall not perish, but have everlasting life." Jesus stepped in between your acts and your accuser and paid your ransom; thus you have been made free.

No matter your sin, fault, or flaw you have been emancipated from the bondages and yoke of sin by the Blood of the Lamb. Christ died that you may live, prosper and be in good health, even as your soul prospers. The God of Truth has redeemed your soul from the enemy. The price for your sin was paid at the Cross. Look behind you no more, press toward the mark of the high calling of Jesus Christ. Learn to focus on the Savior who stands knocking at your door, ready to enter in. Thank God you have been justified.

References: NASB, KJV

Scriptures: Ps 31:5; 55:18; Hab 2:4; Rom 3:23-24, 28; 4:6-8, 5:18-19, 8:33-34; Gal 3:6; Jn 3:16; 3 Jn 1:2; Phil 3:14; Rev 3:20

Keep

Key Scripture: *The LORD bless you, and keep you. ~Num 6:24*

We keep secrets. We keep our word. We keep up with the Joneses and we try to keep the peace. We keep busy and we keep our composure. We know how to keep most things and even some people. Yet no person or thing can keep us like the Lord.

The Bible declares that there is a time to keep and a time to throw away. We must take care to let go of anything that will jeopardize our relationship with God. The Psalmist says we are blessed if we keep His covenants and warns us to keep watch over the door of our lips. Controlling our tongue will allow us to enjoy life and see many joy-filled days.

In Genesis, Adam was to keep the garden, Noah was instructed to keep the animals alive, Abraham was commanded to keep God's covenant, while Isaac was to keep the way of the Lord. In the Psalms, Israel was to keep their tongues from evil and to keep the statutes, ordinances and laws of God. Likewise, in the Gospels, Jesus teaches that we are to keep His commandments and His Word. We are to keep watching and praying so that we do not fall into temptation.

As we are commanded and admonished throughout Scripture to "keep," the Father also promises that as the keeper of our soul He will:

1.   Keep you from falling

2.   Bless and keep you;

3.   Keep you from harm;

4.   Keep and preserve you;

5.   Keep you in perfect peace if you keep your mind stayed on Him;

6.   Fight your battles if you keep silent;

7.   Give everlasting life if you keep His Word; and

8.   Keep you until the end.

We must always be mindful of whom or what is keeping us and where it or they are leading us. Jesus will keep what we permit Him to control. Allow Him to be your Savior, and your Lord. He stands ready to keep your mind, your heart, your thoughts and your flesh. To keep is to watch over, to maintain and to preserve. To keep a thing is to hold onto or control it either physically, spiritually, emotionally, or psychologically. One thing is certain, if Jesus is not your keeper, Satan is.

In celebrating the joy divine in being kept by the Savior, gospel singer/songwriter, Rev. James Cleveland described it best in this hymn, "oh to be kept by Jesus, oh to be His own; kept, to be His forever, kept, to be His alone." Finally, Numbers 6 includes the solemn benediction which perfectly describes how the Father will keep you, the Son will bless you and the Holy Spirit will give you peace. The LORD bless you and keep you; The LORD make His face shine upon you, and be gracious to you; the

LORD lift up His countenance upon you, and give you peace."

References: NASB; ISBE; Jamieson-Fausset-Brown Bible Commentary

Scriptures: Gen 2:15; 6:19; 17:9; Ex 13:10; 15:26; Num 6:24-26; 1 Chr 4:10; Ps 12:7; 34:13; 121:3-4; Eccl 6:3; Isa 26:3; Mk 14:38; Jn 14:15, 24, 1 Pet 3:10

Life

Key Scripture: *For he who finds me, finds life and obtains favor from the LORD. ~Prov 8:35*

Life is a divine and sacred gift. The Word of God is used as its instrument. Life is a choice, whose power is held in man's tongue. It can only be preserved or extended by God. Its days are numbered. Life is a commandment of God and it is one of His blessings of righteousness. Life, both the physical and spiritual, began with the Sovereign God who purposefully and carefully created each of us according to His perfect will.

Life is defined as a general designation of existence. It should be lived with an understanding that it is brief, frail and will come to an end. An age old quip says life is for the living. And indeed it is. It should not be simply passed through without any thought as to what your purpose is. Each of us has been given but one life. Each of us is born with a set time and assignment. If we never discern what our assignment and purpose is, we will always live a very frustrated life. It is up to us to discover, through an intimate relationship with God, our destiny and the imprint we are to leave in the earth.

Your quality of life is directly linked to your obedience of God's laws and dependence on His power. The Father promises not just to give us life, but to give us an abundant life. Simply put, that means we are promised a life filled with heaven's best. Whatever your life may lack, I encourage you to look to Jesus, because He is the Author and Finisher of your faith. He has promised to fill your cup till it runs over.

Yet, we must never assume that an abundant life means a life free of trials, struggles, heartache, or dark days. Rather, the abundant life is one in which we are content in the knowledge that God's grace is more than sufficient for our needs, that nothing can suppress it and that His favor toward us is unending. The Boice Expositional Commentary states that: "Before one can know the abundant life, he must first know Life. That is, he must first be made alive through faith in Christ." Jesus is speaking of this when He says, "I have come that they may have life." It is only after this that He adds, "and have it abundantly." Only when you allow Jesus to be the bread of life that satisfies all your hunger and the water of life that quenches your deepest thirst will you truly live the abundant life the living Word has promised.

Let us understand that life stretches beyond earthly bounds and reaches into eternity. Death, its opposite shall come upon all who remain in Adam (sin); yet to those who believe in Christ is the gift of eternal life. Paul tells us that the wages of sin is death (the natural), but the gift of God is eternal life (supernatural). If you are to receive this new life, you must be born again.

Eternal life must never be confused with mere simple existence, which is what the unsaved are doomed to. Rather, eternal life for those in Christ is the blessed privilege to reign in heaven for all eternity with Christ our Lord; for in Him is life and that life is the light of men. We will finally be connected with Christ, the Chief Shepherd. The promise of eternal life is entered upon on earth through salvation; the payout begins with the return of Christ where you will reign forevermore.

Finally, I admonish you to spend less time securing your earthly life and more time ensuring you have eternal life. For as Scripture says, what profits a man to gain the whole world and lose his soul. What choice will you make today – life or death?

References: NASB; Boice Cmy; NASB Topics; Naves Topics; NLT Verse finder

Scriptures: Gen 2:7; Dt. 30:19; 32:19; Job 33:4; Ps 36:9; 79:11; 102:24; 139:13-14; Eccl 9:9; Ezek 18:19; Amos 5:4; Mk 8:36; Lk 12:20; Jn 1:3-4; 12:50; Acts 17:28; Rom 6:23; Heb 10:38; 1 Jn 5:11

Love

Key Scripture: *This is my command: love each other. ~Jn 15:17*

Oh how I love Jesus is a line in a beloved hymn. Because the greatest love of all is happening to me is part of the chorus of a popular song. Famed soul singer Teddy Pendergrass even sang about a love TKO. In each of these instances, something different is inferred by the word love. But what is love? The true meaning of love, as defined in the Bible, has been corrupted in the usage of modern language and society. Too often, love is confused with infatuation – that elated, "high" feeling we get when we "fall in love." That is not the love spoken of in Scripture.

The Bible interprets love four ways. There is:

1.   Eros which involves passion, sexual attraction and infatuation;

2.   Storge which is a natural affection like a parent for a child;

3.   Phileo which is adoration, deep concern and brotherly love; and

4.   Agape which is sacrificial love wherein you love another, even if they don't deserve it.

The expression "I love you" is frequently bandied about like a puck on hockey ice. We routinely "love" celebrities and famous athletes we've never met simply because they are talented or gifted at sport, song or theatrics. Again, we may ask what does the Bible say about love? Scripture says God is love. It teaches that greater love no man can have than to lay down his life for his friends.

The Bible declares that love is stronger than death and that it covers all sins. Paul says love is patient and kind and lists love as the first of the fruit of the Spirit. There is no fear in perfect love for it casts out all fear. Love constrains us and abounds in us. Real godly love is not static or self-centered. When it is deeply felt, love will cause you to give to the point of self-sacrifice.

The ultimate show of agape love is seen in John 3:16. Love (eros) between a husband and wife is exquisitely displayed in the Song of Songs, Solomon's love treatise. For instructions on how to walk in love, we need only look to 1 Corinthians 13 and Luke 6:35. True love is without hypocrisy and is seen in service to others. This kind of godly love is the binder which holds all other Christian graces in place, for what good is prophecy and gifts if you do not have love.

Simply put, love is the tenet upon which all the law and prophets hang. We must recognize that just as love is the greatest expression of God and His relation to man, so must love be man's highest expression of his relation to the Father, the Son and his fellow brethren. God cannot only be the source of our love, He must be the object. In answering the question, what is love? A theologian said this: love is God's character seen through His grace, recognized in Christ Jesus and manifested in man's redemption. Christ's love is the greatest love of all. Won't you receive it?

References: NASB, Practical Word Studies in the New Testament, ISBE

Scriptures: Lev 19:18; Prov 10:12; Song 8:6; Luke 6:35, Jn 3:16, 25; 13:14; Rom 12:19-20; 13:10; 1 Cor. 13; 2Cor 5:14; 2 Thess 1:3; 1 Jn 4:7-8, 16, 18; Rev 1:5

Mercy

Key Scripture: Therefore let us draw near with confidence to the throne of grace, so that we may receive mercy and find grace to help in time of need. ~Heb 4:16

Mercy is God's compassion, kindness, and concern. What exactly is mercy and how do we obtain it? Once given, is it eternal? And do we really deserve it? We are admonished in Scripture to go boldly before the throne of grace that we may "obtain" mercy and "find" grace. We obtain mercy for past actions; we find grace for the present and future.

Simply put, mercy is when we don't get what we deserve for sins committed against the Father. Mercy is deliverance from judgment. In Lamentations 3:22, Jeremiah says it this way: "It is of the LORD's mercies that we are not consumed, because his compassions fail not."

Mercy is more than a passive emotion. It is offering kindness when you have both the power and authority to execute judgment. Mercy can't be bought, nor can you bargain with God to gain it. The Lord, as the Sovereign Creator has the right to choose to deal with us by exercising compassion (mercy) or wrath (judgment). He "chooses to have mercy on whom He wills." God's choice is based on His eternal and predestined plan for each of us. Where would we be if the Lord judged us according to our sins? We would die; for the wages of sin is death. But thanks be unto God that daily we have renewed mercy because "He does not punish us for all our sins; He does not deal harshly with us, as we deserve."

If we are to receive the Father's mercy, we must be merciful to others. The Bible promises that judgment will be merciless to those who show no mercy. God's mercy to us is made necessary by our need and our sinful nature. Without it, we could never be children of the Father who is in heaven. His mercy is a sign of His faithfulness and covenant. Jesus demands mercy, not sacrifice. Through His act of mercy, we have the gift of salvation and eternal life.

If it is mercy from others you seek, learn to grant it. If you want mercy from God, you must denounce pride, show compassion and repent. True mercy ALWAYS triumphs over judgment.

References: NASB, KJV, NLT

Scriptures: Ps 25:6; 33:22; 106:1; 107:1; 119:156; I Chr 16:34; Jer 33:11; Lam 3:22; Matt 3:21; 5:7, 45; 6:14-15; Lk 1:50; Rom 3:23, 9:15-18; Heb 4:16; Jas 2:13

Name

Key Scripture: *And it shall be that everyone who calls on the name of the Lord will be saved. ~Acts 2:21*

What's in a name? Everyone and everything has one. The Bible says "whatever Adam called each living creature that was its name." A name tells men who you are and may affect how they treat you. It can symbolize strength as do the names Ariel and Aaron. A name can denote fame, "Oprah," or power "Obama." A name may determine your character or destiny. It may be even be an indication of who you are or will become. For example, Abram, Sarai's husband, became Abraham, the father of nations and Sarai, the mocked one became Sarah, the princess. Jacob, the deceiver became Israel, the nation and Saul the persecutor of Christians, became Paul, the Apostle of Jesus.

Hence we see that names are important to people. The Bible advises us that a good name is to be desired more than riches and gold. When someone calls you the wrong name, it says they are not as close to you as a real friend. Likewise, what we call the Lord reveals the nature of our relationship with Him. God's names are dynamic and full of power. He unveils great truths about Himself that are only found in His name. He is Elohim, the creator. He is I AM that I AM, the eternal, unchanging, self-existing One. He is LORD, the self-revealing one. He is Jehovah, the covenant keeper. He is the Alpha and Omega, the beginning and ending of all things.

The Bible tells us we are to hallow the name of the Lord: our Father, who art in heaven, hallowed be thy name. In His name is power, deliverance, salvation, healing, joy, strength, provision, protection, peace, love, counsel, wisdom and guidance – whatever you need is in the name of Jesus. Further, Scripture tells us that the Name of the Lord is:

1.   A strong tower;

2.   Our help;

3.   Excellent;

4.   The only name under heaven by which men must be saved; and

5.   It is the Name above all names

In describing the name of the Lord, two hymns say it best:

There is a name I love to hear, I love to sing its worth; it sounds like music in my ear, the sweetest name on earth; and there is something about that Name, it soothes my doubts and calms my fears.

Remember, that the name of the Lord is above reproach, rebuke and will never need repair. Just as men know you by what they call you: father, mother, friend, pastor, etc, so too can we know the Savior not only by what we call Him, but by what He calls us. For upon salvation, God breathed into us new life and thus we have been given a new name. We are now called the elect of God; a chosen generation; blessed; more than a conqueror; joint heir with Christ; friend of Jesus and finally a Christian. Who do men say that you are when they call your name?

References: NASB, KJV

Scriptures: Gen 1:1; 2:4, 19; 15:2; 17:5; 32:28; 35:9-10; Ex 3:14; Jn 8:58; Deut 28:2-12; Isa 42:8; Prov18:10; 22:1; Ps 8:1;124:8;138:2; Jn15:15; Acts 9:4-6; 13:9; Rom 8:37; Col 3:12; 1 Pet 2:9; Rev 22:13

Peace

Key Scripture: The LORD will give strength to His people; the LORD will bless His people with peace. ~Ps 29:11

Governments hold summits and attempt to fashion treaties surrounding it. Wars are fought in an effort to obtain it. Many have tried to find it in a bottle, through a needle or by other illicit or lustful means. Children have been known to run away from home in search of it. Yet, the peace we seek cannot be found through the machinations of man. It can only be found in Jesus.

Tornados, earthquakes, floods, fires, other natural disasters and end of the world predictions are coming at warped speed. Entire towns have been destroyed in seconds and countless lives have been lost. These calamities bring with them little human explanation or reasoning. As a result what people seek most is solace, comfort, answers and above all peace. In what many consider to be the last and evil days, God has promised us a peace that will surpass all our understanding. To receive it, we are commanded to focus on His Word. We are admonished to seek comfort in Him and not in our own intellect or in the fantastic tales of scientists.

In times of external calm and stability, most people can be at peace. However, it takes an exceptional peace, a supernatural peace, to prevail in the midst of great outward trouble and inner distress. Christ's peace is just that, exceptional, supernatural and divine. As a specific blessing, or gift from Christ, peace is promised to his disciples and all his followers. The peace offered by Christ is unique in that it is everlasting and flawless, unlike the temporal peace offered by the world.

As believers, we are assured of having peace with God as a result of Christ's shed Blood on the cross; peace from God because we are His beloved and the peace of God when we commit all our anxieties to Him in prayer. Further indication of the promise of peace to believers is Christ's speaking the word peace to His disciples just before He was crucified and after His resurrection. In the former He says peace I leave with you; my peace I give you. In the latter He simply says peace be with you.

Imagine peace with God! What a blessed assurance that we need not be troubled or afraid for the peace of the Almighty will surround our going out and our coming in.

Never forget that peace finds its ultimate expression in an intimate relationship with God, made possible by the saving work of Christ. There can never be true peace without righteousness. Peace will never be found in government efforts, through diplomatic "peace" treaties or in the offices of psychologists and psychiatrists. If it is peace you seek, you must first find Jesus. He has promised you peace with the Father, peace with yourself and peace with one another. Remember, the peace of Christ will not only surpass your understanding, it will also guard your heart and your mind.

If we are to receive God's peace, we must first be recipients of His grace. Once you receive His grace, you will receive not just His peace but His love, joy and the sure hope of eternal life.

References: NASB, NKJV; Boice
Expositional Cmy (Grace & Peace)

Scriptures: Ex 40:15; Neh 9:5; Ps 66:5;
99:5; Isa 26:3; Jer 29:11; Mic 5:5; Jn
14:27; 16:33; 20:19; Rom 1:7; 8:31; Eph
4:1-3; Phil 2:2-3; 4:6-7; Col 1:20; Heb 3:1

Power and Authority

Key Scripture: *Behold, I have given you authority to tread on serpents and scorpions, and over all the power of the enemy. ~Lk 10:19*

Often used synonymously, power and authority are not the same things. You may have the power to do a thing, but not the authority. For example, in a court of law, attorneys have power; but the judge is the ruling authority. In the spiritual, Satan has the power to accuse, but Jesus our Advocate has both the power and authority to rule.

Satan can do nothing that the Omnipotent God in heaven does not allow. The adversary's power becomes null and void when compared with the authority of God. The Bible declares that the Almighty Lord is coming with power to rule with authority. The power of God is perfectly displayed in the birth, life, death and resurrection of Christ Jesus. It is that sovereign power that made possible the ultimate authority Christ has over all powers, both human and superhuman. Adonai first gave Satan permission to take Job's belongings and then to touch Job's body, but not kill him. God has not changed; He is the same today, yesterday and forevermore. The enemy can only do to you what God allows.

God the Son operated in that same authority. In His position of divinity wrapped in humanity, Jesus with all power and authority taught, commanded unclean spirits to come out, healed the sick and forgave sins. Because we have been engrafted into God's Kingdom, we have access to the One who rose from the grave and defeated death. We too can resist the devil, lay hands on the sick and speak life because God has bestowed upon us power to exercise authority through Him.

Do you walk in your God-given power? If not, why not? When you speak do demons tremble? They should. Have you laid hands on the sick and they were healed? You can. Why do we faint and retreat with fear when the enemy flares his nostrils and rears his ugly head? We have been given a spirit of power, love and a sound mind. We have been promised the victory and possession of the land. What victories have you lost and promises you have forsaken because you were afraid to use the authority given to you by Christ?

We must learn to speak the word – our tongue has the power over life and death. Exercise it! Stand firm in the liberty you have been given. Speak life to your situation, circumstance or issues. You have been given the power to do so by the ultimate authority, the Sovereign God. Remember, the adversary may have power to touch your life; but he does not have the authority to take your life, for the Lord gives and the Lord takes away.

References: CJB; GW; NASB; KJV

Scriptures: Isa 40:10a;1 Cor. 15:24; Eph 1:21; Rev 13:2; Job 1:12, 2:6; Mk. 1:22, 2:10; Lk. 5:24, 4:36, 9:1; 2 Tim 1:17; Prov 18:21

Praise

Key Scripture: *From the rising of the sun to its setting, the name of the Lord is to be praised. ~Ps 113:3*

Praise ye the Lord. Let everything that has breath, praise the Lord. God is worthy to be praised. These are all familiar and often quoted passages of Scripture. We've memorized them. We regularly recite these and other praise Scriptures in churches the world over every Sunday. Yet, most of us have never given ourselves over to genuine and complete praise – the kind of praise that ignores our fellow parishioners; ignores what family, friends or neighbors will think. I speak of the praise David offered unto the Lord in 2 Sam 6:21.

How do we praise God? The Bible tells us to praise Him with the fruit of our lips, with the clap of our hands, with a dance, with song, with the harp and with the timbrel. Inasmuch as we praise God with dancing, clapping, singing and with instruments, we also praise Him by living a holy and righteous life. God is praised when we obey His laws, statutes, commandments and love our fellow man.

Praise demonstrates our love for and faith in God. It is the outward expression of our worship. Praise will give you victory over your enemy and allow you to have joy in spite of your current circumstance. To praise God is to value Him. We praise the Father for who He is. We thank Him for what He's done or will do. We must understand that worship and praise are not the end result of the Holy Spirit appearing; rather He visits and manifests because we offer up sacrifices of praise. Praise says I believe God, I trust Him and I desire to do His will.

The Bible declares God inhabits or enthrones the praises of Israel. It means He dwells in the atmosphere of our praise. If we are to live victorious and abundant lives, then we must bless the Lord at all times and let His praise continually be in our mouths. Praise agrees with God's perspective and invites the Holy Spirit to work. Praising God for who He is says we recognize His ability to handle any situation we may face. Praise combined with true worship will open your heart. Praise will bring us closer to God's presence.

Praise is more than bodily exercise on Sunday mornings; it is an attitude and a lifestyle. Praise is the response due God for His majesty; it is the dominant characteristic of a true worshipper. We owe God praise. He is praised for His delivering power and because He alone is the Creator and Sustainer of the earth and all who dwell therein. Nowhere is praise more prevalently displayed than in the Psalms. Found within are instructions on how to praise: enter into His gates with thanksgiving and His courts with praise. When to praise, at all times; where to praise: in the great assembly and great expanse; who is to praise: the heavens, all men, angels, the elements and all living creatures, and why to praise: because He is God.

When Jesus is the focus of our praise, we can be like Paul and Silas. They lifted their hearts above the hard place and brought God's power and glory in the midst of their trial. Paul and Silas understood that lodged within praise, prayer and worship were the answers to their deliverance. When praise is really what we do, the presence of the Lord will always be near.

References: NASB; CJB; The Eerdman's Bible Dictionary

Scriptures: 2 Sam 6:21; 20:25; Job 1:21; Ps 21:1; 22:5; 28:1; 34:1-2; 35:28; 66:1; 71:22; 88:10;100:1;119:164;148:1-5; 149:6

Prayer

Key Scripture: *Pray without ceasing. ~1 Thess 5:17*

Believers and nonbelievers do it. Jews and Gentiles do it. Rich and poor do it. The learned and the unlearned do it. Every civilization known to man has a ritual and deity to whom it looks. What is this universal bond of all mankind? It is prayer. Tens of thousands of books are written about it. Innumerable sermons are preached on it and entire conferences are dedicated to it. In fact, from the beginning of time, people have always prayed to someone or something.

Many say prayers, but do not actually pray. For example, the Pharisees were unmatched in their knowledge of Scripture and their ability to say prayers but what they sorely lacked was the insight, instinct and inclination to pray from their heart and spirit, not just their mouth. We must recognize what the Pharisees never learned, that real prayer involves both communion and communication with the Father, not just rote recitation and memorization. Prayer is the human's electrical current to God. It plugs us into His power, His glory and His will. We no longer need the high Priest as in the days of old. We have direct access to God through this marvelous tool called prayer.

Prayer involves far more than talking to God; it requires listening also. Just as we talk to the Father, He longs to talk to us. To hear what He says we must quiet our spirit and mind. When God speaks, it will not be a booming voice as is often depicted in the movies. There will be a stillness and a stirring in your spirit; not a crack from the sky.

Prayer is not a religious form. It is seeking the Lord through an outpouring of your heart and soul. Effectual, fervent prayer depends on God, not self. Though much of prayer is fervent, not all prayer is effectual. There is a mountain of difference. Fervency (the tone in which you speak, the eloquence, the volume of your voice) does not mean effectiveness. Effective prayer is the ability to touch Jesus in such a way that you get a response. Remember, Isa 30:19 tells us, "He longs to be gracious to you and He waits to show His children compassion. For blessed are those who wait for Him." Well like you, the Father shows favor and compassion to those with whom He is in a relationship. That means the only way to know Him is through intimate times spent in prayer. How else do you get to know your friends? You have conversation with them.

Prayer seeks the face of God, not just His hand; for one seeks His presence, while the other looks for His presents. Prayer is not begging. Nor is it just asking and receiving. International prayer leader Alice Smith says, "Real prayer is a vision and voice divine, not a venture and voice of mine." Your prayer closet should be as much a place of observation as it is oration.

As Christians, one of the most important lessons we can learn is how to pray. Prayer is to the soul what breathing is to the body. Real prayer causes God's eyes to open and His ears to be attentive. When righteous men pray with faith and believing, the Father will answer, deliver, heal and save. Real prayer will call forth the earthly manifestation of God's move in the Spirit. It will help us speak the answer, not the problem. Real prayer is not an option; rather it is a necessity and a privilege.

The Model Prayer (Lord's Prayer) found in Matthew and Luke gives the perfect outline and guide on what elements are involved in prayer: adoration (tell God how much you love Him), praise (speaking well of Him), petition (asking God for what you need), thanksgiving (telling how grateful/appreciative you are) and warfare (using the Word as your weapon). The Bible admonishes us to pray without ceasing and in everything by prayer and supplication make our request known to God. Jesus instructs that we should ask, seek and knock. For He declares in John 14 that if we ask in His name, He will do it that the Father may be glorified. He further declares in John 16 that the Father will give whatever we ask in His name.

Real prayer involves intercession for others. We are commanded to pray for: Jerusalem's peace, our enemies, each other and according to His Word. We are charged to pray in the Spirit at all times with perseverance for all the saints. The Bible says we are to watch as well as pray and that we have power and authority through prayer. Effective prayers arm themselves according to Eph 6:10-18. They put on the whole armor of God, by arming themselves with the helmet of salvation, the breastplate of righteousness; they shod their feet with peace and gird their loins with truth. They take up the shield of faith and skillfully use the sword of the Spirit. They recognize that the weapons of their warfare are not carnal, but mighty through God to the pulling down of strongholds.

Prayer is less about the position you pray in than it is about the perspective you pray from and the power you pray to. Prayer, according to noted prayer leader Cindy Trimm, is replacing idle ineffective words with anointed words. 2 Thess 2:8 says that the enemy will be consumed with the spirit of Jesus' mouth (words) and destroyed by the brightness of His coming (anointing). Further, John, in Revelations tells us that we overcome by the Blood of the Lamb and the word of our testimony. What that really means is that we must speak. For we have the power of life and death, blessings and curses in our mouth. What are we to speak ... effective, anointed words that the Lord Himself has spoken? Pray the Word. Why, because in the beginning was the Word and the Word was with God and the Word was God. If we follow the mandate set before us only then can we ask what we will believing that we have it and that the Father will do it that the Son may be glorified.

Finally, prayerfulness or prayerlessness is an indication of the condition of one's soul. Real prayer is discovering God's will, not trying to change His mind. When men pray, destiny is birthed, mountains are moved, lives are transformed, souls are won for Christ and the enemy is destroyed. Know this, if men won't pray; God won't move.

References: NASB; Great Doctrines of the Bible; Great Truth's of the Bible

Scriptures: Ps 34: 4, 6; 55:7; 107:20; 122:6; Prov15:29; Isa 55:11-12; Jer1:6; Matt5:44; 7:7; 16:19-20; 18:18-20; I Cor. 14:15; Eph 6:10-18; Phil 4:6; Jas 1:6

Promise

Key Scripture: *May the Lord, the God of your fathers, increase you a thousand-fold more than you are and bless you, just as He has promised you. ~ Dt 1:11*

We promise to change. We promise to never do it again. We promise to love the Lord. We promise spouses, children and significant others that we will always be there for them. We enter into business deals, get married, accept employment, and buy property all based on a promise. In fact, a great deal of all that we do in life depends on someone's promise. Yet, promises are easily made and just as easily broken and are often subject to conditions and contingencies. But, we thank God that a promise of the Father, is a promise made by the Father. We thank Him that His Word is always yea and amen!

God's promises are gifts graciously bestowed, not a pledge secured by negotiation. When the Father promises, He announces, professes and/or proclaims a thing and it becomes so. His covenants with us contain divine promises to us. For example, the Lord gave Abraham seven distinct promises:

1.   I will show you a land;

2.   I will make you a great nation;

3.   I will bless you;

4.   You will be a blessing;

5.   I will bless those that bless you;

6.   I will curse those that curse you; and

7.   I will give the land to your seed.

What has the Lord promised you? Stand still and watch Him work. Firmly put your feet upon His promises and stay there until the manifestation appears.

The promises of God are His mercies yet received. God promised Noah He would never again curse the ground. He promised David's house would continue on the throne forever. Likewise, He has promised to meet all our needs. Unfortunately, we behave as Israel did, choosing to walk after the world, rather than standing on the promises of the Father. Israel's lack of faith and disobedience caused them to wander 40 years in the desert. Don't let the same be said of you.

Ponder this: if someone offered to pay you $1 million for every promise God did not keep, your payday would never come. The question is not if the promise will come to pass, it is if you believe God to deliver. We are promised that His Word shall never return without completing what it was sent to do. To that end, we have no greater promise than the absolute certainty that through the forgiveness of sin and Christ's shed blood we will have eternal life with our Father in heaven.

Will you be as Abram simply living as a foreigner in the land of your promise or are you Joshua living in the complete fulfillment and purpose of all that God has spoken? Are you possessing the land or living out your days as a sojourner in a tent? Think about it God has promised you rest and blessings with that comes permanence. Have you chosen to roam in the wilderness of disobedience, foregoing the blessings of the Lord to fulfill the longings of your flesh? Moses was in the land of God's promise as a visitor. But he did not possess it as an inheritance.

Look beyond your current struggles and hardships and focus on the promises of God, for they are yea and amen.

References: NASB; NASB Topical Studies; Vine's Word Studies

Scriptures: Gen 8:21-22; 12:2, 7; Num 14:7-8; 2 Sam 7:12-13; Ps 125:3; Eze 37:1-4; Zech 8:1-12; Rom 4:18; 20-12; 11:1-24; Heb 11:9-10; 2 Pet 1:4

Purpose

Key Scripture: *And we know that God causes everything to work together for the good of those who love God and are called according to His purpose for them. ~Rom 8:38 (NLT)*

It is synonymous with foreordination and appointment. Believers are called according to it. Often loved ones don't understand it. Suffering cannot destroy it. Yet, everything and every person created by God has one. It is the reason we were born. We speak of the purpose of God.

Without purpose you will accomplish little in life that matters. Many Christians seem to live more by whim than by a firm determination to pursue the will of the Lord. As God has appointed the elect unto glory, so has He, by the eternal and most free purpose of His will, foreordained all the means contained within. Unfortunately, men often lose or worse, never discover their purpose as the Father has willed and elected it. Some neglect to realize that God's divine plan, purpose or counsel embraces all things, great and small.

The Bible admonishes us to lay aside everything that might hinder us in our purpose and to run life's race with eyes fixed on Jesus, the Author and Finisher of our faith. Because the Father knows the end from the beginning His purpose shall be established and can never be changed. For what He speaks He brings to pass whether it is through you or He chooses another. You must understand that both His purposes and His actions are confirmed by the spirit of his decrees. God is always benevolent in his purposes and conduct, just as He requires His creatures to be. Even though those whom He created are often selfish, and their designs are frequently the direct opposite of the purpose of God. Our calling from God, as Christians, is to become like Christ, not like our friends.

You find purpose in God by obedience. When you follow God's guidance, you know you are where God wants you, whether you're moving or staying in one place. You need not ask Him, what am I to do right here at this stage in my life? His purpose has placed you wherever you are right now. Focus on understanding what that purpose is.

Direction from God is not just for your next big move. You can begin to understand God's purpose for your life by discovering what He wants you to do now. You also find purpose in God by trusting Him to direct your life. Remember, just as Esther was born with a specific purpose, so to have you been born with an assignment. Jesus' purpose was to bear witness to the truth. Like Esther, Moses, Nehemiah and Paul, Jesus fulfilled His purpose beyond what any man could ever imagine. He steadfastly followed the way that God had set before him – the path of the cross.

Whatever purpose God has predestined will occur because He knows the plans He has for you. It will not be by happenstance or by the will of man; but rather it will occur by the deliberate predestination of the Father. Are you prepared to be and/or do whatever it is God brought you forth into the earth to accomplish? Will you die with your intended purpose unfulfilled? Or will you be as David whom the Bible says fell asleep after he had served the purpose of God in his own generation. Will you be as the Pharisees and reject God's purpose for your life? What does God intend to do with, for and through you? Have you positioned yourself in Him in such a manner that He can do it? Seek His face, listen to His voice, follow His instructions and discover your purpose.

> **References:** NASB; Handbook of Bible Application; Finney's Systematic Theology; Boice Cmy; The New Unger's Bible Dictionary; ISBE
>
> **Scriptures:** Num 9:23; Dt 1:1-2; Isa 46:10-11; Jer 4:28; 29:11; Matt 10:29-30; Jn 6:37-38; 18:37; Acts 4:28; 13:26; Rom 8:28; 9:11; Heb 12:2

Satan

Key Scripture: *The Lord said to Satan,*
"The Lord rebuke you Satan! Indeed the
Lord who has chosen Jerusalem rebukes
you. ~Zech 3:2

Is the image of the scary man in the red suit, with cloven hooves, horns, a tail and a pitchfork really the devil? Does Satan look like the many frightening characters we see during Halloween? If none of these images represent Satan, then who is he and why does he put so much fear and trembling in man? Why is he blamed for many of man's foibles, frailties and faults?

We know his many names. But do we really know who he is and how he operates. He is called a deceiver who disguises himself as an angel of light. He is Beelzebub, the father of lies. He is the dragon, the old serpent and the enemy of your soul. He was a former member of the heavenly, angelic host. Lucifer (Satan's original name) was the anointed cherub who was set apart for God's divine purpose. He was created perfect in all his ways, but iniquity was found in him and pride caused his downfall.

Satan is a mystery to most and a myth to others. He is often used as a scare tactic in horror movies or the antagonist in the latest string of apocalyptic films. He is not any of those things. The Bible declares that Satan is 1) a strong man fully armed; 2) the prince of the power of the air; and 3) a roaring lion seeking whom he may devour. Despite who Satan is, Paul assures us that greater is He who is in us than he who is in the world. And Jesus proclaims in Luke that we have authority over serpents, scorpions and over all the power of the enemy.

Understand that Satan is not alone in his spiritual war and neither are you. He has demons and evil spirits; we have God's Word, the blood of the Lamb and the heavenly host. Winning the war means we can never be unaware of Satan's strategy and tactics. Eve was deceived, and as a result, the entire trajectory of the human race changed. Like many Christians, Eve did not know her enemy. You will never defeat an opponent you do not understand.

To effectively wage war against Satan and win, we must have a foolproof battle plan. Next to knowing Jesus and His saving grace, we must know the truth about Satan. Just as we should be as a three strand cord that's not easily broken so too is our warfare threefold: the world, the flesh and Satan. Many are easily defeated by the devil because of the lust of the flesh, the lust of the eyes and the pride of life. We are often too willing to be impressed with our own press. As a result, Satan uses the same tactics – Pride and rebellion – throughout the ages. Sadly many continue to fall prey to his schemes.

The Bible's blueprint for resisting Satan is clearly laid out in Ephesians 6:10-13. We are to be strong in the Lord, put on the whole armor of God and recognize that we do not wrestle against flesh and blood and that the weapons of our warfare are not carnal, but mighty through God to the pulling down of strongholds. Scripture reveals that our battles are not waged in the natural, but in the spiritual realm. Fighting in the natural is futile. We must fight not of our own might or power, but rather by God's Spirit. Remember, God's word cannot return to Him void and He has promised you the victory. Know that the one who seeks to devour you cannot because He was defeated on Calvary's Cross.

Satan can never be God's equal, but he is God's sworn enemy forever. He is and always will be a defeated foe. Resist him and he will flee. Recognize that you overcome by the Blood of the Lamb and the Word of your testimony. Ask yourself: are you Satan's victim or are you victorious through Christ Jesus?

References: NASB; NLT; Boice Expositional Cmy

Scriptures: Job 16:12; Ezek 28:13-15; Dan 10:13; Matt 25:41; Lk. 9:1; 11:21; 1 Pet 5:8; Jas 4:6; 1 Jn 2:15-17; Rev 12:9; 20:2

Sin

Key Scripture: *If we confess our sins, He is faithful and righteous to forgive us our sins and to cleanse us from all unrighteousness.* ~1 Jn 1:9

What constitutes sin? Is every wrongdoing sin? Does everyone sin? Is it possible to live a life free of sin? Does God hate one sin more than another? What's the difference between sin, transgression and iniquity? These are all questions we have either asked or heard. Sin and its consequences are not often preached in church today. Yet, even a cursory reading of the Bible will open your eyes to the realization that there is such a thing as sin, and it is not pleasing in God's sight.

Psalm 51:5 teaches that we were brought forth in iniquity, and in sin were we conceived. Paul calls sin a yoke of bondage and says it will easily beset and entangle us. All sin is disobedience and is contrary to God's will. Galatians 5:19-21 gives a clear description of what sin is. In it we see that following the desires of your sinful nature will result in sexual immorality, impurity, lustful pleasures, idolatry, sorcery, hostility, quarreling, jealousy, unbridled anger, selfish ambition, dissension, division, envy, drunkenness and other sins. We are warned that those who live accordingly will not inherit the Kingdom of God.

Sin is freely chosen. We willingly decide to step outside of the boundaries God has set and walk according to our own design. The Bible reveals that whoever commits sin, commits lawlessness. We have become a people without regard for God or His law. The urge to satisfy our flesh comes before our desire to please God. To sin is to miss the mark. To commit a transgression is to willfully rebel. According to Rebecca Brown, author of Unbroken Curses, iniquity is a residual consequence of sin that affects both the sinner and his seed. Iniquity is driven by a condition of the heart and involves wickedness, unrighteousness, transgression and perversion.

Sin is universal. Sin separates you from the Savior and the wages thereof is death. Sin knows no race, color, creed or socioeconomic status; for all have sinned and fall short of God's glory. Throughout the Bible, we see examples of those who chose to answer the call of Satan and ignore the commands of God. Adam and Eve sinned their way out of the garden. Because of man's unbelief, God caused the entire earth to flood; Sodom and Gomorrah were destroyed by fire and brimstone. Israel wandered for 40 years; Moses never entered the Promised Land. And because of idolatry, both Israel and Judah were taken captive.

But blessed be the name of the Lord. We serve a just God who sent His Son to pay the price no human or animal sacrifice ever could. Scripture says He made Him who knew no sin to be sin for us that we might become the righteousness of God in Him. God so loved us, that He sent His only Son that whoever believed in Him would have eternal life. To overcome the stench, the stain and the sting of sin, we need only repent, confess that Jesus is Lord and believe that God raised Him from the dead. We must accept the gift of salvation freely given by the perfect Sacrifice who hung on the cross, died and rose again. We must look to Jesus, the Lamb who was slain for the sins of the world.

References: NASB; NLT; Unbroken
Curses

Scriptures: Gen 3: 17-24; 6-8; 19:1-23;
Nu 14:18; 20:12; 2 Ki 17:1-24;18; 24:10-
24; Rom 3:23; 2 Cor. 5:21; Gal 5:19: 21;
John 1:29

Temptation

Key Scripture: No temptation has overtaken you but such as is common to man; and God is faithful, who will not allow you to be tempted beyond what you are able, but with the temptation will provide the way of escape also, so that you will be able to endure it. ~1 Cor 10:13

The devil made me do it. I just couldn't help it. Everybody does it. He, she or it looked or felt so good. It was just so tempting. These are phrases we have all uttered to explain away our sin. We sing we fall down, but we get up." We pray "lead us not into temptation, but deliver us from evil." We even promise NEVER to do it again. Yet it seems temptation and its magnetic draw is our faithful and familiar friend.

Temptation is as old as sin. It is first seen in the Garden of Eden where the serpent tempted Eve. Adam and Eve succumbed to the temptation and failed. Jesus was tempted in the wilderness and prevailed. Temptation in its purest form directly challenges what God forbids. It distorts the Father's instructions and denies the truth of His Word. Satan, the tempter, never uses what is unknown or displeasing to tempt us. His foolproof method is still the lust of the eye, the lust of the flesh and the pride of life.

Remember, Satan tempts God tests. Satan tempts not just to make you do wrong; he tempts to cause you to lose eternal life with Jesus. He tempts to destroy; God tests to improve, reprove or approve. God tested Abraham and Job. Satan tempted Eve, the mother of mankind and Jesus, the Giver of eternal life. One brought sin and condemnation, the other brought victory and justification. Satan is the ultimate source of all desire, action and thought that is contrary to God's Word. Eve gave way to the lust of the eye. Jesus resisted the lust of the flesh and pride of life. Heb 4:15 says Jesus has been tempted in all things as we are, yet He is without sin. We must recognize that temptation will always masquerade as what it is not: something good and perfect. Know that because we are brought forth in iniquity and conceived in sin, our flesh is susceptible to fall. Yet we must never forget Paul's assurance in 1 Cor 10:13 that no temptation has overtaken you but such as is common to man; and God is faithful, who will not allow you to be tempted beyond what you are able, but with the temptation will provide the way of escape also, so that you will be able to endure it.

Simply put, we do not have to fall. Jude says, now to Him who is able to KEEP you from falling and present you in the presence of His glory blameless with great joy. A beloved hymn puts it this way: Yield not to temptation for yielding is sin, each victory to help you some other to win. Fight manfully onward, dark passions subdue, look ever to Jesus, He will carry you through. Ask the Savior to help you, comfort, strengthen and keep you, He is willing to aide you. He will carry you through. Know that you can have the victory over sin and temptation. When we yield to temptation, it says we don't trust God. As a result, we fall into temptation which will either develop your character or destroy your soul. You will either learn from it or grow stronger in God, or you will succumb to it and risk eternal damnation. Which do you choose?

References: NASB, Eerdman's Bible
Dictionary; Zondervan Pictorial Bible
Dictionary

Scriptures: Gen 3:1-7; Deut 13:3; Job
23:18; Matt 4:1-11; 2 Tim 2:22; Heb 4:15;
12:4-11; Jas 4:7; 1 Pet 4:12-13;

1 Jn 2:16

Think

Key Scripture: *I know the thoughts I think toward you saith the Lord, thoughts of peace, and not of evil, to give you an expected end. ~Jer. 29:11 (KJV)*

As a person thinks in their heart, so they become. Literally, you are what you think and believe. Your personality is the sum total of your thoughts. You are today what your thoughts, beliefs, and convictions have made you. If your mind is filled with thoughts of trouble, fear, failure, and anxiety, then this will be reflected in what you say, "For out of the abundance of the heart the mouth speaks." Remember, salvation began as a thought in your mind before it ever became a reality in your spirit. The greatest battlefield your will ever face is in your mind.

We cannot separate our thoughts from our temptations. Every fight is won or lost based on what you think. Satan targets your mind and peppers it with lies. You no longer think on those things which are lovely and pure. You no longer meditate on God's word. Instead, you begin to focus on the world and believe that God's will and purpose for your life will not come to pass. But you must stand on Jeremiah 29:11 believing that the Lord knows the thoughts that He thinks toward you, and that you have an expected end.

We must correct our thinking habits, for our thoughts are the seeds we plant in the garden of our mind that will produce the harvest which we will reap. When you think on the Word of God and the things of God, you will begin to see things from a heavenly reality rather than an earthly perspective. As such, you will call those things that are not as though they were. You will activate your faith based on what you think. The result will be you walking in the manifested Word of God and receiving the blessings of God. Allow the Holy Spirit to renew and transform your mind recognizing that your thoughts are bound to follow.

Whatever we think that is not in the purpose, plan and path of God's will for our life will not bear fruit. At least four times in Scripture, we are told that man's thoughts outside of God's will are futile. Do not be deceived by the wiles of the enemy as Eve was. If you do your thoughts will neither be of God or from God. The serpent was able to convince Eve to first doubt God and then deny His Word.

Always remember, what you think determines what you believe. What you believe determines what you say. What you say you will eventually do. What you do will determine your character. And your character determines your destiny. Take care to watch what you think.

References: KJV, NASB, NCV; The Strategy of Satan, Dr. Hobart Freeman

Scriptures: Ps 94:11; Pro 21:7; 23:7, Jer. 29:11; Matt 12:34; Rom 1:21; 12:1-2; 1 Cor. 3:19; Eph 4:17; Phil 4:8

Tongue

Key Scripture: *The plans of the heart belong to man, but the answer of the tongue is from the Lord. ~Prov 16:1*

Words spewed forth from it have wrecked many a home. Untold millions are sent to ruin and despair from it. Churches are divided because of it. Yet, too often people of faith do very little to control the capacity in which they use it. Solomon says the power of life and death lie within it. We speak of that seemingly untamable human organ called the tongue.

Scripture says the tongue does not always speak truth and that it is often used as a sharp sword. Jeremiah refers to the tongue as a deadly arrow. Isaiah likens God's tongue to a devouring fire when it is used in judgment. Conversely, the Father in whom we have belief will hide us from its scourge. James describes an uncontrolled tongue as the companion of a deceived heart. However the tongue of Christians who sincerely walk upright before the Lord, will exemplify pure speech, love and godly character. Solomon declares that when wielded by a wise man, the tongue can promote health.

We must be mindful that even in the midst of crisis, it is imperative that we guard our ways lest we sin with our tongue; for nothing can wreak more havoc than what we say. Understand that a tongue full of poison and used for evil can defile the entire body. As believers we are to be disciplined in our speech if we are to win souls, live holy and model Christ. Moreover, bridling our tongue helps us advance righteousness and God's Kingdom. Hence, we must recognize slander and backbiting as bitter waters which spring from demonic worldly wisdom.

The power and influence of the tongue are disproportionate with its size. Exercising self-control over this small member begins with having a mind that is focused on Jesus. The words we speak probably affect more people than any other action we can ever take. As a result, we find that Scripture continually admonishes us to watch what we say and to let the words of our mouths and the meditations of our heart be acceptable to the Lord.

Proverbs speaks of four tongues: 1) the Controlled Tongue which causes you to know when to be silent, when to give advice and to think before speaking; 2) the Caring Tongue whose possessor speaks truth while seeking to encourage; 3) the Conniving Tongue which is filled with gossip, slander and half truths; and 4) the Careless Tongue which churns out lies, curses and words which lead to destruction and damnation. I ask, from which tongue do you speak?

God in His wisdom left us instructions in His Word of how to use and not use our tongue. We are told to use the tongue to speak justice, sing of His Word, exult and praise Him and confess His Son Jesus as Lord. We are likewise, warned to refrain from using the tongue to falsely accuse the brethren, express rebellion, deceive and lie.

Remember, whoever keeps his mouth and his tongue, keeps his soul from troubles. With the tongue we can both praise God and curse men. We can bind and loose. We can decree and declare. Understand, how we use our tongue will determine the trajectory of our future. As a sail controls the direction of a boat, your tongue controls the direction of your life. Are your words aimed at heaven or hell?

> **References:** NASB; Halley's Bible Handbook; Handbook of Bible Application; Life Application Study Bible

> **Scriptures:** Job 5:21; Ps 14:19 35:28; 39:1; Pro 6:7, 12-14; 10:14; 12:18; 15:23; 18:21; Isa 30:27; Jer 9:8; Jas 1:26-27; 3:2, 5-10

Tribulation

Key Scripture: These things I have spoken to you, so that in Me you may have peace. In the world you have tribulation, but take courage; I have overcome the world. ~Jn 16:33

Tribulation is considered a forceful pressing of one's emotional and mental being. It is the picture of having a heavy weight placed on one's heart and being crushed to the point that you feel you are going to die. It is an unpleasant subject for most Christians to discuss unless they are lamenting about their personal situation. However, the cold reality remains that all people of God will at some point in their walk with the Lord face it. Tribulation will either strengthen you or break you.

In the New Testament, we find that tribulation is the expected experience of those who follow after Christ and believe His Word. Trials and tribulations resulted in all kinds of pressure ranging from the day-to-day aggravations to confronting the most serious afflictions. It was understood, that much of their suffering was at the hands of their sworn enemies because of whom they served. Yet, we, like the N.T saints must understand that although Satan has the authority to defeat Christ-less people, we serve a God who has conquered all his powers.

When adversity hits or afflictions are seemingly never ending, in our distress we may get angry with or question God. It is in the human spirit and nature to ask why. Why God have you allowed this to happen to me? Why now? Why in this manner? Often frustrating is that God may or may not answer and if He does, the answer He gives may not offer any more clarification to your plight. However, we must never lose hope in the Father or in the process. His Word tells us that all things work together for our good because we love Him and are called according to His purposes. We may not understand it or agree with the method, but just know that God's ultimate purpose for us is to grow more into the image of Christ, especially in the difficult and hard places.

At the same time, we cannot make excuses for our times of tribulation when they are the result of our sin. We do serve a forgiving God. And, yes our sins are justified (forgiven) by the Blood of the Lamb. However, that does not mean we do not suffer the consequences of our actions. But, when we are truly justified, trials and sufferings will not defeat us. They no longer discourage and swamp us, or cast us down into the dungeon of despair and hopelessness. Instead, they become purposeful. The truly justified person knows that their life is completely under God's care. The justified Christian knows that God will take the trials and sufferings of this world and work them out, even if He has to twist and move events surrounding you to deliver you.

Scripture says trials develop godly character that will enable us to rejoice in our sufferings. Part of sanctification is going through trials and tribulations. We must be tested and tried that our faith is proved. The true believer's faith will be made sure by the tribulations we experience so that we can rest in the knowledge that not only is our faith real, but so is our God. We are reassured in knowing that because Christ died for us, these light afflictions will not last forever.

In fact, God comforts us and grants us peace during our own struggles in such a divine manner, that we are then able to offer solace to others and tell them of His goodness and grace.

No matter how devastating the trial or tough the tribulation, the right arm of God is mighty and is exalted. He has promised that you shall live and not die to declare His works. He proclaims that though your afflictions may be many, He will deliver you out of them all. He says call unto me, I will give you rest. Be comforted in knowing that unlike with your cell phone connections, where you may hit a bad spot and have no reception, with God there are no dropped calls, only a divine connection. I encourage you with the words of Charles Spurgeon: great trials enable us to bear great joy; and the joy of consolation is in proportion to suffering in tribulation. Be still and know that He is God.

References: NASB; KJV; Boice Expositional Cmy; Practical Word Studies in the NT

Scriptures: Dt 4:30; Ps 34:19; 118:17; Matt 13:21; Jn 10:10; Rom 5:3-5; 8:28-29; 2 Cor 1:4; Col 2:16; Jas 1:2-4, 12; 1 Pet 1:6-7

Trust

Key Scripture: *The Lord is my strength and my shield; my heart trusts in Him, and I am helped.* ~Psa 28:7

Trust is hard earned, easily lost and often nearly impossible to regain. We put our trust in family, friends, jobs, money, material wealth and the government. But Scripture admonishes us to trust in the Lord with all our heart and lean not to our own understanding, but in all our ways, we are to acknowledge Him, for He will direct our paths. David says in the Lord do I trust and walk upright before Him.

To trust is to have an assurance that a person has both the ability and the willingness to come through for you. To trust says that the person or thing we believe in deserves our confidence. To trust a man suggests that we know the man; for it is foolish to trust one you do not know. The Psalmist says some trust in horses, some in chariots, but the truly wise have the Name of the Lord as their defense.

To trust God is to say you have absolute faith in God. To trust Him is often difficult because His ways do not always seem sensible to us. He told Noah to build an Ark when there had never been rain. He promised Abram and Sarai a baby, when each was well beyond childbearing years and never had a child been born to them.

Trusting God says we accept that His ways are not ours and that He is not limited by space or time. Neither is He subject to our whining and crying. We

172

must trust Him because He is the I Am. He is the One who simply spoke and heaven and earth were created.

If we are to completely trust the Father, we must surrender our will, desires, ideas and all that we hope into His hands. The Bible says God knew us before we were in our mother's womb and He knows the plans He has for us. We must trust God, because in Him lies our purpose and destiny; our deliverances, victories and defeat. We will overcome because we choose to trust the One who is our strength and our song. Job put it best, though He slay me, yet will I trust in Him.

To trust Him is to stand, even in the face of great adversity or trials. We must understand that it is our very struggles that the Lord will use to test how deeply we are rooted and grounded in Him. Our faith and trust must be in our hearts, not just our head and mouth. We must trust in the Lord always, for in Him we have an everlasting Rock. We trust because in the Almighty we have an eternal stronghold wherein we can find refuge. We trust Him because He knows the way that we take and His mercy surrounds us.

Is your trust in man who has and will continue to fail? Or is your hope in the God of Your salvation who has promised to never leave or forsake you? Do you trust in the temporal trappings of life, or do you trust in things eternal? Trust God for He is from everlasting to everlasting and throughout all generations.

References: NASB; The Treasury of David

Scriptures: Gen 6-8; Job 13:15; Ps 20:7, 31:4; 32:10; 65:5; 71:5; Prov 3:4-6; 28:26;

Isa 12:2; 26:4; Jer 1:5; 29:11; Nah 1:7;
Phil 3:3-4

Wait

Key Scripture: *But as for me, I will watch expectantly for the Lord; I will wait for the God of my salvation. My God will hear me.* ~Mic 7:7

Waiting is a fundamental part of our lives, whether we realize it or not. We wait in all manner of lines. We wait to be seated in restaurants. We wait for what seems like interminable amounts of time on hold for customer service. We wait for the object of our affections to notice us. Women wait endless hours to pay for a service in salons. People willingly wait outside in intemperate conditions to be the first to acquire a new toy or gadget. We gladly wait when we believe that our wait on things and people in the world is not in vain.

Yet when it comes to waiting on God, we become demanding, attitudinal, impatient and even indignant. We summons God as though we are in control and He is the genie in the magic bottle waiting and biding His time until we loose Him to meet our every demand. Our actions suggest all we need is the blink of an eye or the snap of a finger and the Creator of the Universe will come running at our bidding.

We forget that God is Sovereign. He is King of kings and Lord of lords. Part of our responsibility to Him as heirs to the kingdom is to wait. Part of using the time we have been allotted by God is to wait on His move and instructions. In Israel's early sojourn through the wilderness they learned this lesson. They waited for the pillar of fire by night or the cloud by day before they moved. Their traveling was according to God's timetable, not their own. Notice how God took care of His people, even though the reason they stayed in the wilderness was as a result of their disobedience. My friends, if we would but learn this important lesson that waiting on God is not a waste of time, rather it creates times during which we execute our faith and trust in God.

It is our duty and our privilege to wait upon the Lord and trust Him all the days of our life. Scripture tells us to wait on the Lord and be of good courage and He shall strengthen our heart. By waiting on the Lord, David sustained his faith; Isaiah declared we would gain new strength; and Jeremiah opined that it is good for us to wait on God. Let's be clear, nowhere in the Bible will it say the wait will always be easy, trouble free and without trials or tribulations.

Charles Spurgeon gives us an outline on how we are to wait. He says if we are to wait, we must do it with prayer, with humility, with service, and with expectancy. Waiting requires much patience, faith, hope and belief that God will deliver." Waiting for God is an active display of faith in God during impossible situations. Waiting on God is not only biblical, but it is a necessary part of the Christian life if we are to grow and mature.

As a believer, your position is to wait. While you wait, the condition and posture of your mind must be of good courage. Why? Because God's promised support is to strengthen your heart. And your just reward is to see the salvation of the Lord and the hope of righteousness. Waiting focuses the sense of expectation one has on the object. When one 'waits for a thing, it suggests that you are dependent upon that person or something that the person will do. David's posture in Psalm 25:5 becomes clear to us when He says to the Lord, on you do I wait all day.

Though it is sometimes a long day, we must wait. Remember, God operates outside of time. For Him, 1,000 years is as one day. Though your days of waiting may be dark and you can't see God, feel God or even have a clue as to what, if anything He is doing, I admonish you to wait. Jehovah Shammah, the omnipresent God has not left or forsaken you. He has promised to supply all your need according to His riches in glory by Christ Jesus. Know this, you may think time is running out, but God redeems time (e.g. Abraham was 100 when Sarah gave birth).

While we wait, we must work. We work by serving God. We are to work the plan He has given us. Truly waiting means our very soul anxiously waits in great anticipation of an awesome exhibition of God's grace, glory and power. There is a reward in waiting. Isa 30:18 tells us that the Lord waits on high to show you compassion. Later Isaiah says we will receive the glorious things prepared by God. Psalms 37:9 promises we will inherit the land. Waiting brings fulfillment of His revelatory vision. The Lord assures us in Habakkuk 2:3 that though the vision tarries, wait for it, for it will surely come in its appointed time.

Further, the Bible declares that they that wait on the Lord will mount up with wings as an eagle, run and not be weary and walk and not faint. We are guaranteed salvation if we wait on the Lord and that we will never be put to shame.

We must wait on God because He is the giver of all blessings. We wait on the fulfillment of His Word which only happens in His set time. We wait for His guidance, direction and protection. To wait on God is to live a life of desire towards God. It is to live a life of delight in God. To wait on God is to live a life of dependence on God and a life devoted to God. We wait on God because we have great expectations of Him. Waiting indicates that we believe, trust and hope in God. We wait because we know deliverance can only come by a miraculous manifestation and show of His power and glory. We understand that all that we are or ever hope to be will come because we have waited to see the goodness of the Lord in the land of the living.

If the miracle has not yet come, trust God for He has a set plan and set time to implement His plan for you. We wait on it because we know that the God of the universe, who spoke it, is well able to complete it till the day of Jesus Christ. We wait because He makes great provisions. And we wait because we have great promises. Our decision to wait on God, says we recognize that His timing is not ours even when it seems He is not answering our prayers or doesn't understand the urgency of our situation. My Auntie and grandmother used to say, "You can't hurry God. He may not come when you call Him, but He's always right on time."

Don't be as Saul who was told to wait seven days for Samuel. Because He was anxious and of little faith, Saul took matters in his own hands ... the result ... David became king. (1 Sam 13:8-14). Saul implied that he, not God was in control. But, I say to you that God is worth waiting for. All we need to do is take a look at Job's situation. In the midst of his struggle, Job chose to wait all the days of his life until the Lord changed his situation. The result – Job not only received back all that he had lost, he got double. Never mistake God's delay for a denial. Likewise, never try to circumvent God and do your own thing. As my Auntie used to say "there ain't no good gone come to that." The lesson for Saul, Job and us is that waiting on God prepares us to have our real needs met.

We will never grow weary of waiting on God if we remember how long and how graciously he once waited for us. Wait I say on the Lord. Your set time is nigh. Wait, I say on the Lord and be of good courage and He will strengthen your heart.

References: NASB; CJB; Expository Dict. of Bible Words; ISBE; Handbook of Bible Application; The Treasury Of David

Scriptures: Gen 21:1-5;1 Sam 13:8-15; Ps 25:5; 27:14; 31:24; 33:20; 37:9; 59:1-9;119:74;130:5;Pro 20:20; Dan 12:12; Isa 30:18; 40:31; 49:23; 64:4; Lam 3:25-26; Hab 2:3; Mic 7:7; Lk 8:40; Acts 1:4; Gal 5:5; Rev 17:14

Wisdom

Key Scripture: *For the Lord gives wisdom; from His mouth come knowledge and understanding. ~Prov 2:6*

Wisdom is defined as the infinite, perfect comprehension of all that is or might be as found in God. In its simplest form, wisdom is the ability to discern right from wrong. It is much sought after, often claimed and seldom attained. Wisdom is a divine gift for those who seek the Giver.

If godly wisdom is to be exercised, we must first begin with a fear of the Lord. We must exhibit a reverence for the sovereignty of God and who He is as the creator and sustainer of the universe. Proverbs tells us that wisdom is available to all, but her price is high. Wisdom, understanding and righteousness are intertwined. For the truly wise are obedient to God, patient, reliable, humble, diligent, perceive things as they really are. True wisdom must have God as its center, beginning and ending in Him.

Wise men give the things of God more attention than they do worldly affairs. Wisdom needs God's infinite grace for its cultivation. When man trusts simply in his own achievements and talents he is bound to go awry, for the Bible admonishes us to lean not to our own understanding, but in all our ways acknowledge Him and He will direct our paths. We are warned not to forsake wisdom, because she is our protection. We are to love her, and she will watch over us. The writer of Proverbs tells us that wisdom is more than a thing, she communicates and has character.

Wisdom comes with maturity and trusts in the Lord while knowing His will and His Word. True wisdom does not come from man's philosophies or ideas. In faith, wisdom is ours for the asking. According to Prov 13:20, if you want wisdom, walk with the wise. We must remember, like spirits attract and water will seek its own level. As such, he who has a fool as a companion will thus become and act foolish.

Wisdom is: despised by fools; an attribute of God; more precious than rubies and gold; and has its beginnings and strength in fearing the Lord. Wisdom brings: peace and joy; protection and deliverance; God's favor to your life; and is a reward to all who acquire her . Walking in wisdom will bring us in right relationship with God, with others and with ourselves.

Wisdom brings meaning into our lives and frees us from the vacuum of a life spent toiling for money, power, status or material gain. Is your life filled with the wisdom of God or the folly of man? To the only wise God be glory forever through Jesus Christ. Amen.

References: NASB; NCV; ISBE; The Treasury of David

Scriptures: Job 28:28; Psalm 111:10; Prov 1:7; 3:13-18; 2:5; 9:10; 13:20; Romans 16:27; James 1:5

Worship

Key Scripture: Come, let us worship and bow down; let us kneel before the Lord our Maker. ~Psa 95:6

Worship means to bow oneself down; to lay prostrate. To truly engage in it, one must honor, revere and recognize the superiority of the One to whom homage is paid. It acknowledges the Divine perfection of the Creator. It is born out of praise, thanksgiving and a desire to enter into the inner sanctum of God where He stands ready to meet you. The seraphim and the cherubim's constant cry of holy, holy, holy is music in the ears of Elohim. Worship is God glorified in man's dependence.

Worship can be done anywhere, anytime and by anyone. It may be done with or without singing and music. Real worship is not dependent on the style, volume or speed of a song. Worship must be rendered in spirit and in truth. You must worship with a glad response and your entire being. We should worship with reverence for and thanksgiving to God. We must recognize that God does not need human worship; it is what He desires. Yet, if we are to ever have an intimate experience with the Lord, we must worship and adore Him.

Entering into worship takes preparation. We cannot come before God unclean. In Exodus, God instructed the people to consecrate themselves. We must come before the Throne with a humble heart and great respect for God's sovereignty and power. Worship is a rational activity, not some spooky, unintelligible muttering. Real worship is from inside the heart and is not driven by outside stimulators. Worship is an encounter with the living and holy God and is reserved for Him alone. When we worship we ascribe to the Lord the glory due Him.

When entering the Presence of God, there is nothing we can give Him that He does not already possess. It should be our good pleasure to do as David did, and bring our best gift, our worship. For we understand that worship is not coming to God to get things from him, though we are free to do that. It is not even confessing our sins or pleading for grace, though these flow from worship naturally. It is acknowledging God to be God. It is recognizing you have been invited to have an audience with the King. It means having genuine and sincere worship. It is understanding that it is because of Christ's sacrifice on the cross that we are free to worship.

It ought to be as natural to worship as it is to live, eat or breathe. When we draw near to God, he draws near to us. Worship involves giving God your all. In return, He sups with you. He talks to you. His glory overwhelms and engulfs you. His train fills your temple. One true experience with God in the Holy of Holies and you, like Moses, and the biblical forefathers are forever changed. You will long to stay in that secret place and dwell under the shadow of the Almighty. Your desire will be to continually bask in His presence and be bathed by His glory. Worship the Lord! Worship the Lord, for in His presence is fullness of joy.

References: NASB; Boice Cmy; NASB Topics; NLT Verse finder; Ungers Bible Dictionary; Zondervan Pictorial Bible Dictionary

Scriptures: Ex 3:1-6; 19:10-15; 34:14; Lev 2:3; Dt 6:5; Jdg 17:6; 2 Ki 17:27-29; Ps 2:8; 24:3-4; 27:4, 8; 29:1-2; 147:11; Isa. 66:2; Mic 6:6-8; Mal 3:3-4; Heb 10:1-10; 12;28; Jn 4:21-24; Jas 4:8; Rev 4:8-11

Worry

Key Scripture: *So don't worry about tomorrow; for tomorrow will bring its own worries. Today's trouble is enough for today. ~Matt 6:34 (NLT)*

Are you a warrior or a worrier? One makes you the victim; the other gives you the victory. Do you worship or worry? One brings you close to God; the other leads to despair and destruction. To worry indicates that you lack an understanding of and faith in God's ability to take care of your every need.

Worry is the mind's way of having the illusion of control. Remember whatever controls your mind, controls you. We become what is in our heart. If you fill your thoughts with doubt, worry and anxiety, you will, become a worrying, doubtful and anxious person. We worry, knowing full well we can't change the situation, circumstance or problem. Worrying drains you of energy and of mental and physical resources. Worrying and obsessing about a winter storm or the flu doesn't mean the storm won't rise and you won't catch the flu.

Worrying is a futile exercise. It accomplishes nothing and creates more problems than you had before you began to worry. Your future is in God's hand and He will manage it as He as predetermined before the foundation of the world, whether you worry about it or not. As a childhood song says, He's got the whole world in His hands. My friend that includes you and whatever it is you are worrying about. Worry is a sin. The Bibles says as a man thinks in his heart so is he.

Simply put, if your thoughts are always engaged in worry, your trust level in God is zilch. Worry leads to anxiety, which is contrary to trust and faith. To worry and become anxious suggests we concentrate and depend too much on earthly possessions, connections and influences. When worry anxiety attempts to overtake you. Remember, the Bible admonishes us to pray and wait on the Lord. He didn't say worry while you wait.

You cannot worship God and worry too. If you are worrying, you are not looking to the Father as the Author and Finisher of your faith. What you are saying by your actions is that God, I don't believe you can take care of your creation. In essence, your choice to worry rather than worship and war causes you to slander God as it relates to His wisdom, knowledge, goodness and providential care. If you want to live a life free from worry, put God first. Since we are created to know and serve God, then the only truly successful course in life is to trust Him and not worry.

Do we suppose that Jehovah who created us and redeemed us through the Blood of Christ will not look after us? Let it not be so. When you dwell on the goodness of the Lord in the land of living, you will find peace. Let us be clear, being concerned about something is different than worrying about something. Concern moves you to action; worry immobilizes you and moves you to inaction. We must learn to make the Kingdom of God our main concern, not a second thought.

Keeping things in proper perspective will help alleviate worry. Planning for tomorrow is time well spent; worrying about tomorrow is time wasted. To plan is to carefully think ahead about goals, schedules and trusting in God's guidance. Worrying causes you to be consumed by fear. It causes you to let your plans interfere with trusting God. Worry reveals a lack of faith and will make you forfeit peace with the Sovereign God.

Remember the same God who created your life can be trusted with the details of your life. The Lord does not ignore those whose trust and dependence are in Him. A noted theologian once said; don't let your worries of tomorrow affect your relationship with the Savior today.

References: NASB; Boice Cmy; Handbook of Bible Application

Scriptures: Gen 21:7; Ps 37:8-9; 69:1; Prov 20:24; Isa 40:30-31; Matt 6:19-34

About the Author

Angela Thornton is a writer, speaker, intercessor, trainer and blogger. She teaches a weekly Bible Study each called Wise Word Live. She also writes the Wise Word blog and contributes monthly to Blessed Life Magazine. Angela is also developing the Wise Word Online Bible Study.

She has over 15 years teaching experience in church and faith related settings. Angela will develop and tailor a message that best meets your needs and theme. For requests please contact info@wise-word.net.

Angela resides in Washington, DC with her husband Min. Daniel Thornton. They are the parents of two adult sons.